NEW DIRECTIONS FOR COMMUNITY COLLEGES

Arthur M. Cohen
EDITOR-IN-CHIEF

Florence B. Brawer
ASSOCIATE EDITOR

First-Generation Students: Confronting the Cultural Issues

L. Steven Zwerling
Ford Foundation

Howard B. London
Bridgewater State College

EDITORS

Number 80, Winter 1992

JOSSEY-BASS PUBLISHERS
San Francisco

EDUCATIONAL RESOURCES INFORMATION CENTER

Clearinghouse For Junior Colleges

UNIVERSITY OF CALIFORNIA, LOS ANGELES

FIRST-GENERATION STUDENTS: CONFRONTING THE CULTURAL ISSUES
L. Steven Zwerling, Howard B. London (eds.)
New Directions for Community Colleges, no. 80
Volume XX, number 4
Arthur M. Cohen, Editor-in-Chief
Florence B. Brawer, Associate Editor

Microfilm copies of issues and articles are available in 16mm and 35mm, as well as microfiche in 105mm, through University Microfilms Inc., 300 North Zeeb Road, Ann Arbor, Michigan 48106.

LC 85-644753   ISSN 0194-3081   ISBN 1-55542-731-6

NEW DIRECTIONS FOR COMMUNITY COLLEGES is part of The Jossey-Bass Higher and Adult Education Series and is published quarterly by Jossey-Bass Inc., Publishers, 350 Sansome Street, San Francisco, California 94104-1310 (publication number USPS 121-710) in association with the ERIC Clearinghouse for Junior Colleges. Second-class postage paid at San Francisco, California, and at additional mailing offices. POSTMASTER: Send address changes to New Directions for Community Colleges, Jossey-Bass Inc., Publishers, 350 Sansome Street, San Francisco, California 94104-1310.

SUBSCRIPTIONS for 1992 cost $48.00 for individuals and $70.00 for institutions, agencies, and libraries.

THE MATERIAL in this publication is based on work sponsored wholly or in part by the Office of Educational Research and Improvement, U.S. Department of Education, under contract number RI-88-062002. Its contents do not necessarily reflect the views of the Department, or any other agency of the U.S. Government.

EDITORIAL CORRESPONDENCE should be sent to the Editor-in-Chief, Arthur M. Cohen, at the ERIC Clearinghouse for Junior Colleges, University of California, Los Angeles, California 90024.

Cover photograph by Rene Sheret, Los Angeles, California © 1990.

CONTENTS

EDITORS' NOTES

During the past decade, as educators have attempted to discover the reasons why so many community college students do not complete their courses of study, some have found that many students are caught between two worlds: family and peer groups who often place little value on higher education, and an educational environment with its own very different cultural assumptions.

This volume of *New Directions for Community Colleges* focuses on what is at stake—what is lost, gained, fought for, and given to compromise—when, for the first time in the history of a family, one of its members aspires to a brighter future through education and takes a first step by enrolling in a community college.

The topic is covered in two sections. The first section delineates the cultural issues that first-generation students encounter as they attempt to bridge the worlds of their families and neighborhoods with that of the community college, where so many of these students are enrolled.

The second section describes specific campus programs that are designed to encourage and enable students to overcome cultural barriers and realize their educational goals.

Coeditor Howard B. London brings his perspective as a sociologist to the opening chapter, in which he describes the cultural transformation first-generation students often face.

In Chapter Two, Lois Weis adds another dimension to the cultural conflict by illuminating race and class differences that often exist in the community college environment.

Richard C. Richardson, Jr., and Elizabeth Fisk Skinner, in Chapter Three, find that although the sons and daughters of college-educated parents may be unacquainted with campus culture, they are more likely than minority students to be familiar with the contours of middle-class culture. The authors delineate the marked differences between white middle-class and first-generation minority students in how they identify with their new role as college student.

In Chapter Four, L. Steven Zwerling recounts his own awakening, as a young teacher, to the conflicts of first-generation students and focuses on adult students, providing case histories.

The next two chapters provide vivid and personal case studies. Laura I. Rendón, in Chapter Five, describes her own transformation, from her emergence from a Mexican American, working-class family, through her beginnings as a community college student, to the ultimate achievement of becoming a university professor. She provides insight into the "confusion that arises from daring to live simultaneously in two vastly different worlds while being fully accepted in neither."

Julia Lara's autobiographical account, in Chapter Six, chronicles the confusion and anguish of being caught between her traditional Dominican culture and that of modern American society. As she straddles two worlds, being an outsider in so many realms leaves her with a clouded sense of social and economic destiny.

Beginning with Chapter Seven, we take a look at community colleges that have addressed the problems described above and successfully overcome them. Eduardo J. Padron provides an illuminating look at his own campus, where English is a second language for 65 percent of the student population. Padron describes how programs for recruitment, retention, monitoring, and the celebration of cultural diversity make the college experience welcoming to first-generation students, many of whom are foreign students.

In Chapter Eight, John Chaffee provides a positive look at specific programs that have had impressive results in fostering the development of first-generation and at-risk students to facilitate their assimilation into a college environment. He describes in detail programs such as cooperative efforts with local high schools and others that guarantee admission to four-year colleges. Chaffee shows that colleges that institute programs that teach students to think analytically and communicate well verbally have high success rates with first-generation students.

In Chapter Nine, Wayne J. Stein describes the role of Native American tribal colleges in a people's struggle to better their position in a historically oppressive and hostile society, while at the same time preserving their collective identity. Stein points out that, in addition to an effort by tribal community colleges to develop intervention programs, these community colleges transcend their traditional role with an extraordinary concern for the individual student.

In the final chapter, Peter Nien-chu Kiang provides a comprehensive overview of the problems of Asian immigrant and refugee students. Through numerous student interviews, he delineates barriers such as language, racism, and alienation and suggests the development of Asian-American studies programs as a solution.

Community colleges often provide a beacon of light to potential students from a kaleidoscope of America's cultures, yet their attrition rates are discouragingly high. We hope that this collection of studies will help educators become more sensitive to the cultural conflicts that first-generation students encounter and that it will suggest ways in which they can refine educational practices so that more of these students will be able to realize their dreams.

L. Steven Zwerling
Howard B. London
Editors

L. STEVEN ZWERLING *is program officer for the community college program at* the Ford Foundation *and served as editor of* New Directions for Community Colleges *no. 54,* The Community College and Its Critics.

HOWARD B. LONDON *is professor of sociology at Bridgewater State College and is currently working on two projects—a study of the relationship between family dynamics and what students make of a higher education and a study of the implementation of general education at colleges with limited financial resources.*

*The cultural challenges faced by first-generation students are not
limited to the classroom but include the difficulties of redefining
relationships and self-identity.*

Transformations: Cultural Challenges Faced by First-Generation Students

Howard B. London

At the turn of this century, most college students were white male adolescents and the sons of doctors, lawyers, ministers, prosperous merchants,
and well-to-do farmers. The smaller number of females who went to
college were, with notable exceptions, enrolled in normal schools in order
to become teachers, and they were expected to leave the classroom if they
married. During the following nine decades, the world has become increasingly urban and bureaucratic, advances in science and industry have
changed the face of war and peace, and great migrations have mixed
peoples and cultures as never before. As a result of these and other changes,
the contemporary student, statistically speaking, is no longer upper middle
class, adolescent, or male; instead, the proportion of working-class and
minority students has increased dramatically, older students are now
commonplace, and women undergraduates now outnumber men.

   A disproportionately large number of these "new students to higher
education" are concentrated in community colleges. Any understanding of
their experiences and any programmatic attempts to ease their transitions
into higher education require that their stories, individually and collec-
tively, be placed in the context of the cultural challenges they encounter.
This volume is dedicated to that task.

Social Mobility and First-Generation Students

Most full-time first-generation community college students are the benefi-
ciaries of what sociologists call structural mobility. Typically, their grand-
parents did not finish high school and held blue-collar jobs; their parents,

who also may not have finished high school, now hold either blue-collar or lower-level white-collar positions. As technological advances have made many jobs obsolete and created others and as more occupations have sought to "professionalize" by keeping their recruits in school longer, students have increasingly needed to exceed the educational level of their forebears in order to maintain their relative socioeconomic position. Like a column of marching soldiers, everyone has moved along without getting any closer to those in front. Enrolling in a community college has become a popular and effective way of keeping pace, and families of first-generation students often approve of this means of advancement. Entering a community college does not, after all, entail seeking something "other" but instead builds on a continuous if not fully predictable process of living out the American dream.

However, for many students, going to college holds some surprises. College is, after all, a rite of passage from adolescence to adulthood, and as I have described elsewhere (London, 1989), educational decisions can be mediated by family dynamics. Students (including older students) sometimes find a psychological resonance between their quest for individuation and autonomy and their choice of a major or career. For example, a student may receive pleasure from majoring in a subject that is remote from his or her parents' imagination. This quest for autonomy can take a student further from the family, class, racial, or ethnic orbit than anyone had bargained for. Family forces, of course, are not the only propelling ones; intellectual fulfillment, career preparation, social standing, and financial ambition are part of what is often an ever-shifting hierarchy of motives regarding educational decisions and social mobility.

Whatever the inspiration, for some students, going to college can be an eventful point of departure, one that both prompts and hastens movement into some "other" culture. When this occurs, powerful social and personal dramas are played out, for cultural membership helps define who we are in the eyes of others as well as ourselves, and it does so in the most elemental ways. Indeed, every student making such a transition whom I have interviewed during the past several years has reported having to renegotiate relations with family members, friends, and, in a fundamental sense, with themselves. These negotiations are not always accomplished easily or with a happy ending, for such passages inevitably call into question the very meaning of allegiance and love, over which people can intensely disagree. Thus, upward mobility can produce a discontinuity that arouses feelings of loss, conflict, and disloyalty—as well as of discovery, reconciliation, and joy (Stierlin, 1974).

Though the cultural content may vary, such struggles are reported by students of diverse backgrounds, whether white working class, African American, Native American, Hispanic, or Asian. If there is a common element in their poignant stories, it is that these students live on the margin of two cultures. Park's (1950) definition of marginality applies here: these students live and share in the life and traditions of two distinct cultures, never quite wanting or willing to break with their past, even if permitted to do so, and never fully accepted, because of prejudice, in the culture in which they seek a place.

Socialization into the Middle Class

Max Weber, whose turn-of-the-century writings have deeply influenced modern conceptions of social class, noted that money by itself is rarely an effective claim to social position. Indeed, pecuniary claims are usually seen as pretentious or crude and often further exclude the parvenu from the group to which he or she aspires (Weber, [1946] 1968). What is important for membership in a status group—Weber's terms for a collectivity that has successfully claimed a certain social esteem—is appropriate cultural expression. "Above all else," he wrote, "a specific *style of life* [is] expected from all those who wish to belong to the circle" (p. 932, emphasis in the original). Weber's definition of style of life included "all the perceptible differences in the *conduct of everyday life*. Of special importance are precisely those items which may otherwise seem to be of small social relevance, since when . . . differentiation is concerned it is always the conspicuous differences which come into play" (p. 390, emphasis in the original). He also noted that "all those things [which distinguish ethnic groups] we shall find later on as objects of specific differences between status groups" (p. 391).

Among the everyday, seemingly insignificant badges of status-group membership that Weber discussed were language (including vocabulary and accent), social conventions and rituals of all kinds, patterns of economic consumption, understandings regarding outsiders, relations with outsiders, and matters of taste in clothing, food, grooming, and hairdo. Students, it should be noted, extend Weber's list of status-group insignia to include tastes in music, sports, cars, and recreation. These items, in other words, are part of the substance or content of a status group's culture, and thus they inform its members of the group's boundaries. Those who take on the culture and its symbols are themselves taken on as insiders, though if they do not share the same ethnic, racial, or religious heritage they may not be seen as full members. Conversely, if one repudiates or otherwise casts off the symbols of membership in one's status group, one risks being held suspect; one may be seen as putting on airs or showing just how weak or false one's allegiances really are.

All this is not to imply that upward mobility is the primary goal of first-generation students or that they are ambitious social climbers. In my research, I have found that these students vary considerably in their feelings regarding mobility. Some cherish it, others are wary of it, and still others see it as incidental to other goals. However, once students find themselves being resocialized into a new status group, the meaning and expression of status-group membership inevitably becomes of great concern to them. In the absence of more direct conversation, students inevitably feel compelled to gauge the reactions of friends, family, and even themselves to the changes they are making, and they do this by "trying on" or experimenting with displays of cultural symbols and artifacts that are associated with some other status group.

Moving up, in other words, requires a "leaving off" and a "taking on," the shedding of one social identity and the acquisition of another. Usually this is a slow, incremental process, consisting of subtle and often tentative innovations in the conduct of everyday life. This image is consistent with the formulations of Erving Goffman (1959), a micro-sociologist who wrote with an extraordinarily observant eye about how people "present" themselves to others. According to Goffman, people reveal much about themselves, intentionally or not, that influences how they are assessed by others. For students and their families and friends, these displays are a potential lightning rod for anxieties regarding the extent and direction of change, and whether old relationships have eroded or been betrayed. Furthermore, students are often aware that such displays can be provocative, and some consciously devise performances for family and friends that are calculated to address, however indirectly, some of their deepest concerns regarding separation and social mobility. Such "discussions" are reported by students as having an electric quality to them, as if everyone knows something is going on just beneath the surface. For example, one student orchestrated a seemingly casual but really planned use of her new taste in music (acquired as a result of a course initially taken to fill her schedule):

> It's really hard for me at home. It's like living in both worlds. I come here and I'm one person, and I go home and I'm the other person that they knew, but not really. I think everybody is kind of wary and leery of me—my younger brothers, my sisters, my father and mother, old boyfriends, or people I still socialize with when I go home. It's not the same, because, well, I'm not the same. . . . It makes it real hard. The other day I put some classical music on the radio *on purpose*. I like it, and I put it on in my room once in a while, but this time I was in the living room. *I wanted to see what would happen.* First thing I get is someone says, "Shit, oh, Jesus, you're going to go to poetry readings next, ooooh! We won't be able to talk to you anymore." My sister, she really went nuts. There were a couple of friends there, too, having fits. They were looking at me, like "What's the matter with this kid?" [emphasis added] [student interview, May 1987].

This student was not saying that classical music is unappreciated in the working class from which she comes (or for that matter that it is appreciated by most college students) but rather that among her family and friends she suspected it would be taken as a sign of her breaking away. Wanting to check on the possible consequences of this breaking away for her relationships with the people for whom she cared, she staged "evidence" of change that as it turned out ratified her fears: people were "wary and leery" of the changes and, more specifically, of losing her. ("We won't be able to talk to you anymore.") Here is another, less premeditated example:

> I have sometimes said something that I learned at school, and my mother would shoot me a look. [Imitates his mother:] "My, my, my." But I know she is very, very proud of me. . . . [Later] They want me to go on to [a four-year] college from here [a community college], but I know I'm not supposed to become a four-syllable kind of guy. This is not something they would want to see. I think they are envious of the people who are moving into our neighborhood [then being gentrified], but they also just don't like them, and they tell me not to become like them. "Don't let success go to your head, don't be snotty or a jerk." Right? But I think I am changing, that I already have, and sometimes they see that. Maybe they see it better than I do [student interview, Apr. 1990].

For other students, clothing (such as a tweed sport jacket with elbow patches), food (health food and granola, in one case), or ideology (becoming more liberal on social issues than family or friends) became the symbol of separation and mobility. It is not that tweed jackets, granola, and liberalism are the province of the middle class or of college students but rather that family members seize on conspicuous changes in a student's self-presentation in order to express their concerns. In other words, such changes subtly marked the separation of students from their past, both in their own eyes and in the eyes of those who still inhabited that past, and everyone seemed to know that this was the case. Thus, these presentations of change were also, in effect, a careful feeling out of possible changes in people's ways of caring and not caring for each other. (A sensitive description of separation from the past and the emotional tribute it can exact is Richard Rodriguez's (1982) autobiography, *Hunger of Memory*.)

Self-presentation on campus can also be problematic for students, even when in the company of other first-generation students. For example, one student self-consciously tried to change what she called her "harsh way of speaking and my 'dems' and 'dose.' " Another stopped wearing the black clothes that were so popular among her friends at home but that, she said, were an embarrassment on campus. A student who started carrying a briefcase was teased mercilessly by his classmates who thought he appeared too studious. For some students, then, the ease and matter-of-factness of social life cannot always be taken for granted; this is, perhaps, a feeling familiar to immigrants, to people who have had to "fake it" the first few days on a new job, or to guests at a formal dinner who have no knowledge of proper conversational topics or of which fork to use first.

Sometimes, of course, the face grows to fit the mask, and the role once played converges with the self one has become. A student I followed over her four collegiate years (the first two in a community college) spoke to this point. She laughed at herself as she recalled:

> I didn't look like college material. [Said with mock snobbishness:] "I didn't talk like it." All those other kids had new clothes. They—I don't know, they were just different. Shiny teeth or something. Probably because no one ever in my whole family or any relative I know about had ever went past high school, and it just seemed like that wasn't for me. [Said with awe:] College! It just seemed to me like a dream, a place I just didn't go to. Like I didn't have the brains, for one thing. It cost a lot of money, for another thing. [Laughingly:] I really thought you had to have all these brains or whatever to go to college. And look at me now. [Pointing to the logo on her blouse:] Who would have thought I'd be wearing a preppie alligator? [student interview, Apr. 1986].

Conclusion

College changes all students, whether first generation or not. Sophisticated and useful surveys have documented changes in students' psychological and ethical development, attitudes and beliefs of one kind or another, ability to think abstractly and critically, and so on. These changes have been attributed to exposure to the curriculum, continued maturation, "readiness" for college, the quality of teaching, as well as other factors. While some students experience a dramatic falling away of scales from the eyes so that the world is seen anew, for most students changes are more modest and incremental. It is evident, however, that for many first-generation students (especially those who declare a liberal arts course of study or who transfer to a baccalaureate college), the very act of going to college indicates an interest in attaining a white-collar, middle-class position not previously attained by a family member, and this may take the student into uncharted cultural territory.

In the innocent belief that mobility is unproblematic, students are often unaware, at least initially, of its potential costs in personal and social dislocation. It soon becomes apparent, however, that old relations are changing and that new ones must be forged. It is only when we see that negotiating cultural obstacles involves not just gain but loss—most of all the loss of a familiar past, including a past self—that we can begin to understand the attendant periods of confusion, conflict, isolation, and even anguish reported by first-generation students.

References

Goffman, E. *The Presentation of Self in Everyday Life.* New York: Doubleday, 1959.

London, H. B. "Breaking Away: A Study of First-Generation College Students and Their Families." *American Journal of Education,* 1989, 97 (2), 144–170.

Park, R. E. *Race and Culture.* Glencoe, Ill.: Free Press, 1950.

Rodriguez, R. *Hunger of Memory: The Education of Richard Rodriguez—An Autobiography.* Boston: Godine, 1982.

Stierlin, H. *Separating Parents and Adolescents: A Perspective on Running Away, Schizophrenia, and Waywardness.* New York: Quadrangle/New York Times, 1974.

Weber, M. *Economy and Society: An Outline of Interpretive Sociology.* (E. Fischoff and others, trans.) New York: Bedminster Press, 1968. (Originally published 1946).

HOWARD B. LONDON is professor of sociology at Bridgewater State College and acting director of the higher education doctoral program at the University of Massachusetts at Boston.

The cultural issues at urban community colleges involve tensions between middle-class and poor students of the same race as well as between students of different races.

Discordant Voices in the Urban Community College

Lois Weis

This chapter examines cultural issues in the context of the urban community college. There is no question but that students, most of whom are first-generation college attenders, encounter cultures in these colleges that exist in at least partial conflict with the cultures of their family and neighborhood. London's (1989) path-breaking work employs the psychoanalytic and family systems theory of Helm Stierlin (1974), combined with the life history approach, to detail the sometimes irreconcilable differences that first-generation college students experience. The "breaking away" of London's men and women of various ethnic groups is reminiscent of that of the young man from a mining family in Bloomington, Indiana, who, in the film *Breaking Away,* manages to enter the culture of university students through his participation in a bicycle race. As we all know, perhaps from personal experience, "choices" between conflicting cultures are not easy, no matter how inspired or motivated we are. Many of us have had to "break away" in one form or another, and we know firsthand the pain of culture clash and the loss that accompanies such moves, whether they have involved class, racial, ethnic, or gender issues.

Thus, the work of London and others on this subject is enormously powerful. But cultural conflicts exist not only between the school and the home or community; there are also discordant or nonsynchronous voices *within* institutions and communities. These voices cannot and should not be ignored; they reflect the historical struggles of communities at the same time that they serve to maintain tension between and within communities.

Data regarding these "voices" were gathered during a one-year ethnographic study, for which time several assistants and I acted as participant

NEW DIRECTIONS FOR COMMUNITY COLLEGES, no. 80, Winter 1992   © Jossey-Bass Publishers

observers in a school I will call "Urban Community College." The college is located on the edge of the urban ghetto in a large northeastern city—a city on the brink of deindustrialization. The college serves predominantly a poor black population and, to a much lesser extent, a poor and working-class white population. It is largely oriented toward the liberal arts but also offers a number of vocational programs such as child care, criminal justice, radiological technology, and secretarial science.

The voices we heard were rife with tensions—tensions that must be understood and contextualized if we are to comprehend the experiences of those who proceed through or fall out of our institutions. This chapter focuses on three axes of tension: those between black and white students, those between the black middle-class faculty and the black urban poor students, and those between black male and black female students. All these tensions are present on the campuses of our urban community colleges. All are powerful and deeply rooted in the struggle for a better life.

Though the focus here is on black students, class and gender struggles also exist within white communities. However, whites were a minority on this campus and, as such, tended to band together as a group, thus concealing the tensions that characterize the broader white population. For whites, the constructed "other" was black. For blacks, the "other" was white to some degree but also included those of the opposite gender or different social class.

On a theoretical level, the work of Emily Hicks (1981) and Cameron McCarthy (1990) on nonsynchrony is exceptionally illuminating. As McCarthy argues, the relations among social class, race, and gender in schooling are more complex and potentially contradictory than is suggested by either liberal or conservative discourse on these issues or even by the newer parallelist theory in cultural studies. Both Hicks and McCarthy propose that the operation of race, class, and gender relations in schools and other institutions of family, society, and economy is systematically contradictory or "nonsynchronous," rather than parallel or symmetrical. Indeed, the position of Hicks and McCarthy is that "individuals or groups, in their relation to economic, political, and cultural institutions such as schools, do not share identical consciousness and express the same interests, needs, or desires at the same point in time" (Hicks, 1981, p. 221). Consequently, the dynamic relations of race, class, and gender do not reproduce each other but instead lead to "interruptions, discontinuities, augmentations, or diminutions of the original effects of any one of these dynamics" (McCarthy, 1990, p. 85).

Data presented in this chapter illustrate the validity of this "non-synchronous" position. The discourse of college students and faculty reveals that different race, class, and gender groups have qualitatively different experiences in schools and that these groups exist in fundamental tension. This tension should not, however, be seen as occurring only on site. It is rooted in the historical trajectory of different groups as they move through American society. It is to these tensions of race, class, and gender that I now turn.

Tensions Between Black and White Students

At Urban Community College, there are few overt tensions (expressed in fighting, racial taunts, and the like) between black and white students or between students and faculty of different races (Weis, 1985). Instead, tensions are expressed through separateness and, especially on the part of the white minority at the college, through criticisms of black students. These tensions, of course, are informed both materially and discursively by a larger society, which has historically constructed blacks as "other than" and inferior to whites and whites as "other than" and superior to blacks. Neither group, of course, has totally accepted its constructed position. The black community has struggled for hundreds of years to break both the material and discursive practices related to race in the United States, and it has been joined by factions of whites at various times. By no means has the hegemonic definition of race been uncontested or static.

The historically rooted tensions between blacks and whites are primarily played out around the open admissions policy of Urban Community College. All applicants who have high school or general equivalency diplomas are admitted and become eligible for financial aid packages. More than 90 percent of the students receive some form of financial aid, and 87 percent receive Basic Educational Opportunity Grants (BEOG) of about $500 per semester plus tuition. It is often alleged by both faculty and white students that many (particularly black) students are "there for the money," since the dropout rate in any given semester is exceptionally high. My observations as well as official college data indicate that only about half of any class completes the course work each semester. The absentee rate is similarly high. For example, a fashion merchandising class began in the fall with close to thirty-five students; by December 14, between seven and twelve students were attending regularly. Attendance at a business seminar declined from thirty-two to between four and eleven by the end of the semester.

White students are particularly critical of this "problem." While some of the white students receive BEOG, virtually all black students do; therefore, in the eyes of white students, it is a distinctly racial issue. The following example is from an informal discussion:

CAROLINE: . . . I don't like the kids who come to school, get their BEOG checks, and they don't show up. . . . You don't see them until next semester.

CYNTHIA: . . . I don't think they should be accepted back into school next year. Now I understand they have phony proof, that kids were collecting under phony names and stuff. I heard a rumor—you know the machine downstairs that takes pictures?—that somebody came in and took a bunch of pictures and picked up [other students' checks]. Whether it was true or not or whether that was rumor, I don't know. But when you first go to school the classroom is completely filled. Now I'm lucky if I have twelve students in class. My biggest class there's about twenty students. And if there's any kind of money distributed, after that three-quarters of the class is gone.

JENNIFER: I was in a minority—I was paying for my education. A lot were getting EOP [Equal Opportunity Program grants]; a lot were getting BEOG. . . . I wanted to be there. I cut my classes here and there, but I would generally attend my classes. But there would be some classes where there would be six students in there once the money came in. . . . A lot of kids really came out well. They get tuition, spending money, textbooks, and transportation, so they were really *making* money by going to school. . . .

   You find a lot of people who go to school because it's worth their while. This creates a lot of problems because you get into some of the classes and they really don't give a darn; they don't really want to be there, and it makes it really difficult for you sometimes because I was paying enough money where I didn't want to waste the time.

. . .

JOANNIE: [I would change] the students themselves. They're here just for the money or they're here just to, you know, to be with their friends. . . . I think it's just a big joke with some of the people. They're not here for an education. I was doing some transcripts in general studies [she is a work-study student], and there were people who took five courses and passed one. . . . One took six and failed all six. It was terrible. They're not here for an education. They're just here for the fun of it.

LW: . . . In child care [the curriculum she is in], do you feel this?

JOANNIE: Yeah, like we have a test, OK. Most of them don't show and then they have an option of taking a makeup. But they even miss the makeup day, too. It doesn't bother them. . . .

   I'm work-study. They [other students] got their grants and I'm still waiting for money from work-study. . . . As soon as the BEOG and TAP [state Tuition Assistance Plan] come in, they leave. *They cheat me* [emphasis added]. I'm working for my money and it bothers me. . . . They're giving the school a bad reputation. . . .

   My studies here are so easy for me. Child care doesn't require much from students. It's nothing. I haven't had homework in the last three or four weeks. It's just like high school to me. . . . In math I just sit and do my homework in class.

White students, then, are angered both by the high rate of absenteeism among black students and that so many black nonattenders receive grant monies. High absenteeism is taken as a lack of seriousness, which whites feel gives the school a bad reputation and necessitates slower-moving classes. Whether this gives the school "a bad name," as Joannie argues, or like Jennifer, they feel "I was paying enough money where I didn't want to waste the time," the opinion that they are being cheated by black student behavior is deeply embedded within many white students' identity. As a distancing device, it enables these students to feel different from and superior to the black students; they pay, they are serious, they want to move quickly, they do not want to waste time. (While some black students, particularly the women, also complain about high absenteeism on the part of their peers, they do not express the same bitterness as do white students and, for the most part, do not feel that *they* are being cheated because of others' absence.)

Although whites center many of their comments on grants, the issue of money does not fully account for the discourse on difference. Many white students, too, are grant recipients. As the following comments suggest, white students also focus on the perceived low level of academic skills and lack of effort among blacks.

JULIE (a fashion merchandising student): There's one thing that really bothers me [about Urban College]. I'm very upset by it. I can't understand why they allow people that don't even know how to multiply four times six into school. There's a girl that was in my class, and one day I was sitting across from her and she asked me how much four times six was. I mean that was such a blow. I still can't understand why they let people come in that aren't ready.

. . .

BARBARA (a secretarial science graduate): That is the thing that stands out most in my mind—that the majority of the people could not read—they couldn't read. I was very shocked; I just couldn't believe it. . . . They couldn't read a page out of a book without it taking them an hour.

LW: . . . Did you know white students who couldn't read also?

BARBARA: No—there was one girl that seemed to be having a hard time, but I don't know if it's that she just didn't understand what was going on.

LW: Did you feel that this slowed down the classes you were in?

BARBARA: Yeah, it did. . . . The courses went *very* slowly; that's about what it came down to.

LW: . . . Were your friends black, white, or both?

BARBARA: The majority were white. I wasn't close with any of the black students.

LW: There wasn't much mixing between black and white students?

BARBARA: Not really. . . . There wasn't any hostility; it was very casual. You're in your own little cliques.

. . .

JOHN (a liberal arts graduate): In several cases I sat next to people who couldn't spell their name, and they were working on their second year of an associate degree. . . . Most of the time you could walk through the halls without even seeing anybody. It was not an overcrowded school by any means. But two days out of the year . . . was what they called "EOP Day." You couldn't even move in the school. You couldn't move because there were so many people swarming. . . . It was like somebody opened the doors and people started rushing in. It was certainly an absenteeism school where most of the people there were not there. . . . I would have to say that in large part it was a big waste of taxpayers' money. I don't think that anybody should be paid to go to school if they're not going to go. . . . If you're going to go to college you should get something out of it, and I don't think they did.

JAN (a business administration graduate): I found that I was one of the few people there that actually did any work. . . . The other students didn't bother to do the work. . . . The work had to be a lot slower.

. . .

DICK: The RT (radiological technology) program was an advanced course; in fact, you had to take four exams before you could even get into it [the RT program was virtually 100 percent white]. . . .

The other classes were mostly empty; in fact, they were mostly scatter-brain type courses. . . . I think Urban College is a below-standard school. I think that is because of the socioeconomic level of the community that is supporting the school—that is basically the black community here. . . . They lower their standards to accept most of the blacks. . . .

A lot of the students come from the South; I think they're getting a free ride. They go and they get all this money from BEOG and TAP and everything else.

Clearly, white students react negatively to constructed elements of black student culture, and they define themselves as different from it. Many feel that students are "just there for the money," that they disappear after "checks come out," and that they put little effort into schooling. While most of the white students are not so brazen as to talk about black students as a whole in these terms, some are:

DICK: The radiological technology [program] was sort of a clique. . . . As far as the other students, considering that the majority of them were black—we really don't associate with them. . . . Culturally they were behind us. There was a big cultural gap.

LW: What do you mean by cultural gap?

DICK: Well, I worked in California. The blacks there are highly civilized. When I came back here, I found that the blacks were uncivilized. It was really kind of a surprise to me because I had been away from it for a number of years. The blacks out there I could relate to as a person. When I came back here, it was sort of a cultural shock. . . . I've been back here for five years; I'm becoming sort of a bigot myself. The southern blacks came up here and brought up a lot of their culture. I find it very degrading. They're slow in action, slow in moves, and always lagging behind. The American thing is sort of to move up and improve yourself. Basically, from what I see from the southern blacks, they don't care.

While Dick is particularly outspoken on the issue of race, racism runs like a fine line through most discussions with white students. They take great pains to point out that they are different from black students, whom they see as lazy and wasting "our time."

I have suggested that a fundamental tension between black and white students unfolds within the urban community college along the lines of white students' racism. Although I heard occasional comments relating to racism in the college and the society at large among black students, there is no comparable elaboration among the black students in relation to whites. There are, however, tensions relating to both class and gender within the black community itself. It is to the first of these that I now turn.

Class Tensions Within the Black Community

Black students and black faculty are quite critical of each other. While on the surface this may appear to be evidence of a normal set of antagonisms between students and faculty, similar criticisms are not voiced outside of the race and class configuration outlined here. In other words, the tensions are not between students and teachers generally at Urban College but, rather, between black students and black faculty, which suggests an underlying class tension. I will explore the student response to faculty first.

CLIFTON (a business administration student): I noticed that about a few black teachers here, Mr. _____, Ms. _____ at times, too, they try to be more hard on you, try to make the course more difficult.

LW: Why do you think that is?

CLIFTON: Well, I think the simple reason is that they feel they are trying to bring up the education to a better level, but I think they shouldn't be difficult, that difficult. I can deal with that, but not that difficult as far as making the corrections, but having to type it, you know, I'm not no great typewriter [sic]. I have to pay somebody. You just make the course difficult, that what's a pain in the butt. We had workbooks for Ms. _____, never use them, but we're going to pay our money. That's stupid, but I feel that the black teachers, they don't understand it or something—and really disheartening, you know.

LW: What about the white teachers?

CLIFTON: Yeah, they teach on a smoother level, because they, how they outline their course, it's simple, you can grasp it.

While many students express some generalized resentment toward black faculty for being "too hard," George, a former business administration student, takes a different position. He probes beneath the surface of the level of difficulty and criticizes black faculty for being too individualistic—for divorcing themselves from what he sees as the black collectivity, the black community as a whole. The tension between the black urban poor experience and social mobility as represented by Urban College is apparent here. George is, by his own admission, closely aligned to what he calls the "village [ghetto] economy." He is critical of the "black educators" (whom he variously calls the "intellectuals" or the "bourgies") who "don't care about people cut from the cloth—like me, I'm cut from the cloth." He perceives a distancing on the part of the black middle class from the concerns and fears of the underclass and considers this selfish. As he states, "they want to stay comfortable," have their wine and cheese and their nice homes, and ignore what he sees as a return to slavery:

> Every black person in this country is only just 100 years from slavery. They all have poor relatives and people who live in the rural South or urban ghettos. They know what the streets are like; they [the intellectuals] just don't want to deal with it. They have too much to lose. I really believe that soon you'll have a small black middle class, and the rest of the blacks will once again be slaves. Give them a guaranteed annual income and you have a class of slaves; people who have no say in their lives, [who] just can be herded around like animals. We're moving toward that now. Most of these people [in the village] have no basic skills; they can't read or write; they can't do math; they don't know anything about their history; they just don't know. . . . I'm continually shocked.

For George, the class tensions are powerful. While his comments may not be representative, he is able to articulate the reasons for the class tension that I feel underlie black student-faculty relations. These tensions are equally powerful for the middle class:

PERCY (an English professor at Urban College): [When you first start teaching at the community college,] people kind of assume that because you're black or minority that you can relate instantly to minority people. I could relate on different levels, but educationally, it was very difficult. They [students] didn't have the skills I thought they should have. . . . I just assumed certain things even though I was teaching some remedial type of course in composition here.

LW: What did you assume?

PERCY: I assumed that they could at least write sentences, that students had some idea of grammar. I assumed that they knew something about their own history. I would say, you know, Martin Luther King or Malcolm X. They would look at you like "Who's that?". . .

The matter of being scholars, too. I guess I'm somewhat of a scholar, and I guess I try to project that onto my students—to be excellent in what they do. In fact, that is what I always say the first day of class—that you will be excellent and you will do very good in the class. I didn't realize that some of these students had no orientation in studying or in being a scholar or being intellectually curious. That's sort of disheartening.

LW: Do you still find that people assume that because you're black you have some kind of understanding?

PERCY: Yes, [and] obviously I do have a link. Having been born in the South and grew up on the east side of _____, of course I have it. But I also have other kinds of training and background. . . .

Students get the impression that you are not *supposed* to know or do that [appreciate Mozart, enjoy caviar]. You know, "You're like us and why can't you give us a break?" . . . They look for the break in terms of "don't be so hard on us because you understand that we come from this poor background and we are so destitute" and so on.

I tell them, "Bull." Don't tell me about poor backgrounds; don't tell me about walking the streets; don't tell me about drugs and all that kinds of stuff. I've seen it and I've been there. You don't *know* prejudice. I *know* prejudice. I knew prejudice in the forties and fifties—I'll tell you about prejudice. You have to make it on your own. You are really responsible for yourself and you can learn.

LW: What is the response to that?

PERCY: "Yeah, but you made it." "Yeah, and I'll tell you *how* I made it. My mother scrubbed other people's floors while I took care of the other three kids . . . she went out to the suburbs and scrubbed floors. I washed dishes in the city's restaurants for about two years; every summer I worked in a drugstore, paid my tuition to [the state college] myself, so don't talk to me about that. I don't want to hear about that.

LW: When you were talking about "Hey, you're just like us, give us a break," is that the reaction of men or women or both?

PERCY: The men more than the women, and I find black men, unfortunately, have an attitude of "give it to me." . . . "Man, I'm trying to make it and this world is terrible, especially on black men." I've worked it out somewhat. The kinds of societal pressures on black men as we know in America, in their wanting to make it, but more than that, their . . . feeling of wanting gratification now. They don't think in terms of deferred gratification because we have been taught as black men that tomorrow is not promised; you gotta do this *now*. The men are more apt to want to do it now; therefore they're more inclined to want me to give them a break now, slide them through now because they had a jail record or that sort of thing, and that's not stereotypic because a lot of black men do have a jail record. They come from the ghetto.

Percy argued that black students, particularly males, expect him, as a black faculty member, to "understand" their background and "give them a break," "slide them through." Percy's response embodies a spirit of individualism; he argues that the individual can always "make it" if only he or she is willing to try hard enough. This is not to suggest that Percy is unaware of structural barriers for blacks. Any black American knows full well the extent of racism in the United States, but as Percy stresses, individuals have the potential to escape the urban underclass. Percy resents being "hustled" by students and responds by being even more rigorous than many of the white faculty. Thus, there is some truth to the accusation of Clifton and others that black faculty make it more difficult for them. Carl, a black physical education instructor, takes a position similar to Percy's. He, too, is critical of underclass students and is particularly critical of the widespread practice of bringing young children to class when there is no child care available.

CARL: The only thing that drives me crazy is women who bring their kids to class [this is an exceptionally widespread practice]. Why don't they hire a baby-sitter or put them in a day-care center?

LW: Maybe they don't have the money?

CARL: Yeah, that might be true. I feel sorry for the students here. They just aren't motivated. They don't want to learn. If you really *want* to advance, you can. They play jive man in high school and don't get skills.

LW: What motivated you?

CARL: Sports. I loved sports and realized that I'd go no further than high school sports if I didn't do well in school. So I worked. I was motivated; these students aren't. . . . All six kids in my family got a college education.

LW: Did you go to school in the city?

CARL: No, are you kidding? I went to school in the suburbs. My parents moved out of the city so the kids would get a better education.

The class tensions are clear here. Percy, Carl, and others tug in one direction, while Clifton, George, and others tug in another. The middle-class faculty feel that they have worked hard to get where they are and that the students are not serious. The black student underclass feels that faculty are not taking enough responsibility for them now that the faculty have made it themselves.

Gender Tensions

I have suggested that tensions exist within the college along class and race lines. It is important to note here that black students rarely criticize whites. Rather, the focus for their criticism tends to be middle-class blacks or, as this section examines, one another. Generally, black females criticize black males in much the same way as white students criticize black students. In other words, black females suggest that the men are not serious, that they are just there for the money, that they take little responsibility, and so forth. The expressed tensions, however, do not in any way address the issue of a racist society that may have helped to create them.

Men and women in the urban ghetto, like men and women elsewhere, experience different realities. Joyce Ladner (1972) in her excellent study of black women argues that most black females view the duties of the woman as those associated with keeping the home intact. These include caring for children, cleaning house, and providing financial support. Black women are expected to be strong and expect themselves to be strong, and parents (particularly mothers) socialize their daughters with this end in mind. As stated by a female business administration student at Urban, "the women work harder than the men; they've been liberated a long time. Black women have had to be serious—the men have not." Black women perceive themselves to be both the primary care giver to children and the breadwinner of the family. The position of black males in the economy has made it difficult for black men to achieve. Racism ensures that black men have not held patriarchal power, and black women do not see "being taken care of by a man" as a viable option for their lives.

That the desire to provide a better life for children constitutes the major reason that black females attend Urban College and, furthermore, that there is an underlying current of antimale sentiment is clear from the following excerpts from field notes:

After public speaking class Eloise and Jessie were talking about the required speech, and Eloise said she was nervous about giving speeches (she had just given hers). Jesse asked her what the speech was about, and she said it was about their—why they are at Urban College and what they want in the future.

Eloise said she wanted a better life for her and her daughter [in the speech she had said that her "nine-year-old daughter is the most important thing in the world to me"]. She wants to take care of herself—"don't trust no man." Yeah, Jessie agreed, "They keep running out; you got to make a better life for yourself."

ODESSA (a twenty-five-year-old single mother of three): [Going to college] turned me against the wrong crowd. Before I was, you know, with people who really didn't care about their education, but now since I've been going to school, I've been with more people who did care about their education and their futures. . . . It keeps me alive.

LW: If you had not gone back to school, what would you be doing?

ODESSA: Well, I'd probably be goin' out all weekend, . . . just wastin' my time, not really gettin' anything, you know, playin' around. I'm more settled now than I ever was—settled in my mind, not in material things.

LW: So coming back to school allowed you to meet other people like yourself?

ODESSA: It allowed me to keep going, instead of going back to doin' nothing, sittin', waitin' on some man, or something like that. . . . Most of them [young people] think that some man is going to do it for them. I know that if you don't do it for yourself, there's no man that is going to take all the weight off of you. Most women already have children and that causes a little bit of confusion because if the man scolds the child, she'll say, 'You're doing that 'cause he's not yours.'

LW: . . . I've noticed that in school the women seem more involved in their studies than the men do. Am I wrong about that?

ODESSA: No, I think you're right. 'Cause most of the time the men will be in the hall and the women will be in their classes.

LW: Why is this?

ODESSA: I don't know. I really don't talk to many of the men. There's not many that I see that might hold my interest.

LW: See, I've noticed that, too. The men and women. There seems to be a real separation.

ODESSA: To me it does. Even in class most of the men sit on one side and the women sit on the other. . . . Usually I'm by myself. See, most of the women have someone to help them, and I don't [she has no family in town]. My mind is not on fun and games at the time. My mind is totally into what the teacher is saying.

Not only do women perceive themselves as being more serious than men but the faculty also perceive them in this way. In the words of a black social sciences instructor:

EBOE: The women just see the world as being against them, so they have to study more. They just know. Most women today want to stand on their own two feet. They don't want to depend on some guy to dish out $500 to them whenever he pleases. The only avenue to do that is to work hard. Most of the guys here are trying to be slick.

LW: Now, you said that the black women feel that the world is against them so they work hard. The black men ought to feel that way, too. Why don't they?

EBOE: They ought to feel the same way; they don't.

LW: Why?

EBOE: I'd like to know why. I ask them, "Don't you know that things are rougher out there now than ever before? You've got to work harder!" That is strange and it is distressful.

LW: When you say the men are busy being slick, what do you mean by that?

EBOE: Well, if there's a test tomorrow, they would rather go to a party. Many girls would say, "No, I'm going to sit down and study." Many of the guys think that having a good time now is more important than postponing it for some [other] time.

Vivian, also a social sciences professor, stresses the pressures that she feels lead to differential behavior.

VIVIAN: I find that the majority of the females are more serious about the whole thing [school]. I have had some very good male students, but when you take them as a group, I'd say the majority of the women are far more serious.

LW: Why?

VIVIAN: I don't know if it's because of the school situation where people believe that the females are more serious, whereas men are involved in more things in the school—more games or being cool or whatever. Women can show a seriousness and not be mocked and laughed at, whereas some of the men in the culture say, "You're in school, ha, ha, ha. You're serious about this thing! Ha, ha, ha."

You have to be able to take the jazz as a guy. I think that the ones [black men] who have risen to the top have been the ones who have been able to overlook and overstep this "Hey-you're-serious-about-this-whole-thing" image. But you see, you have to be able to balance being cool with being serious in school, and some people can't handle the balance. You can still be a member of the peer group and kill the teacher's exam. Get an A constantly but still come back to hang with the guys and say cool things, but you've got to be able to handle it. Some people can't. . . . Women don't have to hang out and be cool. They, of course, have their children and their household, but that's inside and you can glance at the book every once in a while. I don't think women are nearly as pressured as the men around here.

Some faculty, such as Vivian, are slightly more sympathetic toward men than Percy or Eboe. Others are more sympathetic to the fact that women bear virtually sole responsibility for raising the children, thus making it difficult to attend to their studies. There was general agreement, however, among all the faculty members and women students interviewed during the course of this study that women are more serious about their studies than men.

Thus, the same tensions that exist between black and white students exist to some extent among blacks at the college. The black middle class sees the underclass students as being lazy, just there for the money, and so forth. Women, to some extent, see these same negative qualities in the men.

Conclusion

It is noteworthy that students rarely challenge the racism of the society at large or even the possible racism of white faculty and administrators. Black students are indeed critical, but the criticism is directed at targets within the black community—the black middle class, the black underclass, the black male. These criticisms are not unlike those voiced by white students. When these data were gathered, there was no existing social movement that might serve to redirect these sentiments. In other words, there was nothing comparable to the civil rights struggle of the 1950s and 1960s that encouraged people to focus on an unequal system as the root cause of felt problems. Instead, these students were left with anger that became directed at other members of their race. There was no alternative discourse that might mobilize the sentiments of both blacks and whites who might be willing to break with hegemonic notions of race.

I have demonstrated here the utility of examining multiple voices in the urban community college. Such explorations allow us to focus on the tensions and on the historical reasons for these tensions in our educational institutions. Ultimately, they enable us to understand more clearly the experiences of those who live and work within our society.

References

Hicks, E. "Cultural Marxism: Nonsynchrony and Feminist Practice." In L. Sargent (ed.), *Women and Revolution.* Boston: South End Press, 1981.

Ladner, J. A. *Tomorrow's Tomorrow: The Black Woman.* Garden City, N.Y.: Doubleday, 1972.

London, H. B. "Breaking Away: A Study of First-Generation College Students and Their Families." *American Journal of Education,* 1989, 97 (2), 144–170.

McCarthy, C. *Race and Curriculum: Social Inequality and the Theories and Politics of Difference in Contemporary Research on Schooling.* Philadelphia, Pa.: Falmer, 1990.

Stierlin, H. *Separating Parents and Adolescents: A Perspective on Running Away, Schizophrenia, and Waywardness.* New York: Quadrangle/New York Times, 1974.

Weis, L. *Between Two Worlds: Black Students in an Urban Community College.* Boston: Routledge and Kegan Paul, 1985.

LOIS WEIS is professor of sociology of education at the Graduate School of Education, State University of New York, Buffalo.

Helping first-generation minority students achieve degrees may require nontraditional strategies at community colleges, as well as at baccalaureate institutions to which students may transfer.

Helping First-Generation Minority Students Achieve Degrees

Richard C. Richardson, Jr., Elizabeth Fisk Skinner

This chapter offers the perspectives of recent African American, Hispanic, and Native American baccalaureate recipients on the personal, educational, and societal variables that contributed to their decisions to persist in school and graduate. Our data were derived from 107 in-depth interviews with graduates of ten public universities. The institutions were Brooklyn College; California State University, Dominguez Hills; Florida International University; Florida State University; Memphis State University; Temple University; University of California, Los Angeles; University of New Mexico, Albuquerque; University of Texas, El Paso; and Wayne State University. Case studies of these institutions and a description of the model developed to explain the outcomes are available in Richardson and Skinner (1991). More than half (52 percent) of the interviewees reported attending a community college. A majority of the graduates (58 percent) indicated they were the first in their families to attain a college degree. First-generation college graduates were significantly more likely to have attended a community college (60 percent) in comparison with those who reported that one or both parents had graduated from college (42 percent), but clearly community colleges played an important role in helping both groups obtain their baccalaureates. The stories these graduates told provide valuable insights into the issues institutions must address in order to provide optimal environments for the success of all first-generation college students.

How Students Differ

Many of the prescriptions for improving minority achievement are based on excessively simplistic perceptions of who minority students are. Our

New Directions for Community Colleges, no. 80, Winter 1992 © Jossey-Bass Publishers

research (Skinner and Richardson, 1988; Richardson and Skinner, 1991) reveals a rich diversity of student profiles that can be described in terms of three important dimensions: (1) *opportunity orientation,* the beliefs students develop about valued adult roles and about the part played by education in structuring access to those roles, which in turn are reflected in motivation and goal setting (for a related discussion, see Ogbu, 1987); (2) *preparation,* which involves both the development of expectations about higher education and participation in experiences that approximate going to college (Attinasi, 1989); and (3) *mode of college going,* which distinguishes between students who follow traditional full-time patterns of college attendance and those who enter college with adult roles and responsibilities.

Differences in opportunity orientation, preparation, and mode of attendance influence the degree attainment and transfer rates for all students but have a particularly strong effect on African Americans, Hispanics, and Native Americans because they are more likely to be first-generation college-goers. Hence, they are less likely to understand fully the relationship between higher education and desired careers, less likely to have experienced detailed preparation, and more likely to attend in nontraditional modes.

Opportunity Orientation. The graduates we interviewed knew that as minorities, they had "beaten the odds" in attaining a college degree and invariably attributed their success to "determination." Unlike many of their contemporaries, they understood the connection between a college degree and their potential for a "good" job. Those who came from college-educated families had always believed college was the route to employment opportunity, while many, but not all, first-generation college students adopted this belief later in life as a result of experiences in the workplace or the military. The desire for a good job was directly associated with obtaining more money, security, and power. Several graduates expressed this connection succinctly: "I think my incentive is greed—money and power," said one. "I want better employment, more money, a better standard of living, and more independence," said another. A third said, "I'd like to make a big salary."

A good job was also associated with social status and life-style. Comments such as these were typical: "I'm not a blue-collar type. I'm better than that." "I didn't want to be a common laborer." "I want to live life the way I wish." "Jobs with a degree carry a little more weight than just a job." A college education meant freedom and equality. "You just want to do as much as everyone else does—to be considered intelligent or able to function in society. As a career, of course, yes, that's true, but even just in everyday life, a man with a college degree—it says something," said one African American graduate.

For most graduates, the opportunity provided by college was the primary basis for judging its validity. Students devalued "just going to college" as drifting. They advised future students to have a strong goal and not to worry about whether they liked the experience itself or whether they encountered discrimination.

Yet many first-generation graduates remained somewhat skeptical about the opportunities associated with college. Some came from communities where a college education was not an important element in becoming an adult and were discouraged by the stories of college graduates who returned home to find no employment. A Native American student described the situation on her reservation: "They told you to go to school and you did. You come back with all the education to work for the tribe and help your people, but there are no jobs."

Others, confronted with examples of discrimination in hiring and promotion, were uncertain whether college could overcome the negative effects of minority status. An African American student commented that he had seen white friends in his company promoted over him even though they "couldn't touch me in academics or experience. Those kinds of things bother me," he said, "but then, I think, that's society."

One first-generation African American graduate reported that his family and friends continually told him that he was wasting his time, that the education would do nothing for him. Though he doubted the financial rewards involved, he nonetheless persisted. "I had intrinsic reasons for going, and at times when you're getting negative vibes from everyone you know, you've got to keep your eye on what you're doing."

Preparation. Perhaps the most often cited reason for underachievement is lack of preparation. The graduates we talked with explained their difficulty or lack of difficulty in getting a degree in terms of the adequacy of their preparation, but their treatment of the issue was broader than the usual discussion of academic background. From a student perspective, preparation involves complex cognitive, physical, and social aspects of the college-going experience (Attinasi, 1989). Graduates emphasized the importance of developing accurate expectations about course content and about necessary academic skills as well as readiness for the more general cognitive development usually associated with a college education. Students from college-educated families experienced continuity from their previous learning experiences.

"When I took my first freshman classes in chemistry and math, it was like my junior year in high school. I didn't have to crack a book," said one Hispanic graduate.

"I had really advanced English classes in high school and I knew how to write a paper, a decent paper, and I could do very well, whatever kind of paper they wanted me to write," an African American graduate said.

First-generation college-goers, however, described disorienting experiences: "When I got there [the campus], the things other kids knew already and you're expected to know, I didn't know," said a Cuban American graduate.

"I found that some of the things I should have learned I hadn't. I had to learn while I was in college. . . . There were voids I had to go back and fill in. For two or three years, it's double time," reported an African American graduate.

"It just seemed like we had gaps. It was like we were missing part of the picture. . . . The teachers are saying, 'Remember when you learned this?' and I never missed school but I kept thinking, 'Gosh, did I miss some lectures along the way?' But I didn't; they just were not there," a Mexican American graduate said.

Students usually discussed the physical aspects of college attendance in terms of time. In this study, as in our previous research (Richardson, Fisk, and Okun, 1983), talk about time and schedules was pervasive and revealed the degree to which students were prepared for the demands of going to college. While first-generation students struggled to gain control of the temporal aspects of their experience, students from college-educated families had developed clear expectations about how time should be managed. One Hispanic graduate from a college-educated family found that "college reminded me a lot of my high school, just the way my daily schedules were set up."

Students' preparation for the economic realities of college life also differed. Those from college-educated families had information about sources of financial aid and clear expectations about how to make ends meet, while first-generation college students did not.

Graduates emphasized the importance of demystifying the bureaucratic and academic aspects of a large institution, which they found intimidating, confusing, and impersonal. For example, services like financial aid or those of the registrar's office seemed inaccessible because of puzzling paperwork and long lines. Furthermore, many felt that busy faculty and academic counselors weren't anxious to "waste time" with students. "Nobody wanted to help you; they saw you as bothersome." One student recalled that academic advising was "just a matter of going and telling them the classes that I was going to take, and they signed me off and I went down the road." Even when more sympathetic sources of academic and social support were available, students found them hard to locate. In addition, students often failed to take advantage of information about services because they felt somehow disconnected from the campus. "I think the publications of the newspapers and the board, the 'pin-ups' that you see, you have a way of separating yourself from them. You don't really ascertain them as being seriously intended for you," said one Mexican American graduate.

Students also complained of large, impersonal lecture courses with little student participation and little interaction with faculty who might have "five office hours for several hundred students." The size and competitiveness of some institutions made it hard to make friends; students were hesitant to help each other because they wanted to protect their own standing. While most students are critical of these conditions, first-generation students are at greater risk because they are less well prepared to cope with them.

Through interaction with college-goers and experience with special programs, students from college-educated families and some first-generation students had gained an understanding of how to participate in the complex college environment, but the adjustment was still difficult. An African American student with college-educated parents commented on this inadequacy in his otherwise excellent preparation: "Nothing in my past academic history would have prepared me for the overwhelming factor of being a number; nothing prepared me for that."

First-generation students frequently described their first exposure to the campus as a shock that took them years to overcome. Many minority students were also unprepared for the racial or ethnic isolation—even alienation—they would experience in predominantly Anglo institutions, a finding well supported by previous research (Kleinbaum and Kleinbaum, 1976; Madrazo-Peterson and Rodriguez, 1978; Suen, 1983; Dawkins and Dawkins, 1980). The graduates we interviewed frequently talked of feeling isolated, especially when they had been among a small minority on the campus or in a particular discipline. An African American graduate remarked that there were few blacks in his major: "For the time I was an English major, there were many times that I was the only black person in the classroom. . . . I don't know whether I'm better off for the experience or not or what I got out of that situation, if anything. It just struck me as strange."

From the student perspective, preparation to attend a predominantly Anglo institution is directly related to family educational experience. Students with the most accurate and detailed expectations came from families where a tradition of going to college already existed. An African American graduate recalled the lifelong influence of his mother's college experience on his goals: "[My mother] had encouraged us and prepared us for college from day one. She was a degreed individual so that was always something in our minds."

Preparation was also affected by association with present and past college-goers in school, the community, and the workplace. Positive models helped students prepare for the college experience by providing indirect simulation of college attendance through the stories they recounted. One African American graduate, for example, recalled high school teachers who told him "about the real world, how it really is in college."

The more experience that was shared and the more recent the stories, the more specific and accurate expectations became. A Mexican American graduate explained how his example had helped his brother: "He has taken the initial steps after having seen me do it. He has received the identical scholarship. He is studying [for] the identical degree, and he has the same plans that I have—even the same professors. . . . I think the difference it has made for him is that he has realized that these goals are attainable. I was kind of a trailblazer for him."

Preparation was enhanced by experiences that approximated college going. An African American graduate reported an easy transition from high school to college: "It wasn't much change to me. I was in a lot of college preparatory classes in high school, and they basically tried to get us ready for going to college."

Another graduate found military experience helpful: "I had been used to going to classes in the army, and by the time I got to college all the new concepts and new materials I was getting from my courses weren't alien to me anymore."

Our data demonstrate that many minority students are well prepared for college, and many others can overcome the handicaps of inadequate preparation. While it is difficult to do "double time" to fill in preparation gaps while simultaneously trying to keep up with classmates, minorities, like other first-generation college students, can meet this challenge. Institutional success in helping first-generation minority students succeed is significantly related to prevailing values and attitudes. When minority achievement is both expected and valued, institutions act in ways that allow preparation problems to be addressed effectively. Preconceptions about the limited potential of minorities, however, can turn into self-fulfilling prophecies, restricting the achievement of all minorities regardless of preparation (Richardson and Skinner, 1991).

Mode of College Attendance. The issue of minority achievement is further complicated by the fact that African Americans, Hispanics, and Native Americans are more likely to attend college in nontraditional ways, while current retention strategies are based largely on traditional conceptions of college matriculation (Tinto, 1987).

The striking contrasts between traditional and nontraditional modes of college going evident in our data illustrate why differential access to one mode over the other has significant consequences for success and why support strategies based on the traditional mode are ineffective for nontraditional students. Most well-prepared minority students attend four-year colleges directly after high school. First-generation college students with high opportunity orientations are also likely candidates for this traditional mode of college attendance.

The first-generation college students who began their higher education in community colleges, however, typically attended in nontraditional modes and maintained significant outside roles and responsibilities. Their college going was characterized by shallow connections with the college and by extensive connections with the workplace or the home. For these students, being a college student was just one and often not the most important of many roles. As one African American graduate commented, "I was a full-time student, I was employed full time, and I was a full-time daddy and husband."

Many first-generation participants did not immerse themselves in the student role, partly because it was not well accepted among their reference groups. Their college experience was less intensive and less continuous. Because of multiple responsibilities, students were more likely to attend college part time, to transfer, and to stop out one or more times.

Through our interviewees' descriptions of their complicated daily schedules, we learned that many spent relatively little continuous time as students. Rather than organizing their time around the student role, they attempted to fit a new activity into a familiar time frame, often performing astounding temporal balancing acts. "Getting up at 6:30 to prepare and go to school, taking my son to day care, going to school from 8:00 to 12:30, working on one job from 1:00 to 4:30. Going home . . . Then I would leave at night going to my night job," explained one African American graduate.

Nontraditional students had minimal physical involvement with the campus, coming almost solely to take classes. They knew only a small part of the campus and had little involvement with instructors or other students. They did not participate in student activities or use student services other than the financial aid office, the registrar's office, and perhaps a tutoring service if it were uniquely suited to their needs. They had no time to "hang around" the campus. In fact, spending time on campus was associated with problems—parking, transportation, inconvenient scheduling of courses, and paperwork errors. From the comments of many graduates, we gathered that attending with such limited involvement was not considered to be "regular" college going.

Low Expectations and Academic Achievement

The graduates we interviewed recalled incidents that revealed the low expectations held for minorities by some faculty members. The expectation that minorities were not knowledgeable or capable sometimes caused them to be treated with disrespect in the classroom. "There were so few of us there, and then sometimes in the classes, I mean honestly, you could hear the racial undertones. . . . Most times it was just in the air," said an African American graduate.

Another graduate recalled an African American student in her business communication class who was not afraid to speak up: "[Other students] would treat him, you know, like 'you must be stupid for saying that,' and sometimes their whole attitude would show through after class where there might be sound effects at something he said. You know, he had every right to say what he said. . . . He was made to look ridiculous. It made you feel that what you said didn't matter, you were ridiculous for being in there, and 'we don't need you here,' and so forth."

The most serious problems arose when low expectations were reflected in instructors' grading practices. "I had one instructor who gave me a C because she thought that most blacks needed C's and that we're used to getting C's. I had to go to the ombudsman several times, and not only with her but with other instructors, just to get the grades I deserved. She had given me a D because my paper sounded too good. It didn't sound like something I could write. . . . So I had to go back, get all my sources, come in, and show her where I got every bit of information, where I analyzed it, that it was written nowhere, before she would change my grade. This woman is saying that I couldn't write," reported an African American graduate.

These accounts are reminiscent of evidence reported by Ogbu (1978) that both African Americans and Mexican Americans are graded unfairly in public schools. In his study in Stockton, California, Ogbu found a tendency for African Americans in public schools to be given a grade of C regardless of their individual efforts or progress, a practice he saw as mirroring the situation in the community where African Americans were not hired, paid, or promoted according to their abilities.

Research on college attrition indicates that when discrimination is "overbearing," it becomes a major reason for dropping out for a significant proportion of African American college students (Western Interstate Commission for Higher Education, 1973). Low teacher expectations for minority student performance have also been documented in the public schools (Bennett and Harris, 1982; St. John, 1975; Rist, 1970). Detailed analyses of classroom interaction show the consequences of low expectations: teachers pay less attention to students from whom they expect little, interact with them less, and place lower demands on their performance (Brophy and Good, 1974; U.S. Civil Rights Commission, 1973). Students act accordingly, low self-expectancy results, and performance is impaired (Haynes and Johnson, 1983; Wheelis, 1982).

Dissatisfaction with the social and emotional environment is also a frequently cited reason for minority students leaving college and for poor performance (Tracey and Sedlacek, 1987; Gilmartin, 1980). Like others, we found in our interviews that these noncognitive factors affect minority students regardless of their academic ability or the level of education their parents achieved (Oliver, Rodriguez, and Mickelson, 1985).

Strategies for Success

The first-generation students we interviewed had been successful, despite inadequate preparation, nonspecific opportunity orientations, non-traditional modes of attendance, and debilitating low expectations, because of their own coping strategies and because of the ways that institutions changed to make their environments more receptive to student diversity. We consider first the ways in which students coped.

Student Strategies: Scaling Down. While many students spent relatively little time on the campus, most reported that it had still been important for them to reduce or "scale down" the physical dimensions of college attendance—that is, to find places where they could study, meet friends, or seek support, spaces that provided some measure of "comfortability." The spaces could be almost anywhere on campus—for example, a student lounge or cafeteria, the office of a student support service, or a specific academic department. They also found ways of scaling down the social dimensions by identifying some community of trustworthy and supportive people on whom they could rely.

Cognitively, successful students found a focus and direction for their studies within a diverse university curriculum. Socially, they formed relationships with instructors, identified mentors and advisers, and developed support networks with fellow students (Astin, 1968). Other strategies of successful students—whether used alone or in combination—included using special support programs as a focus around which they could reduce the overwhelming complexity of university life. Students from college-educated families attending in the traditional mode sometimes focused their involvement around a work-study job, membership in a student organization, or, on residential campuses, membership in a dormitory or social organization. Most commonly, however, students centered their experience around the department of their major. Departments were especially important for first-generation students attending in nontraditional modes because their connections with the campus came primarily through course work. For them, departments often provided all the services they needed—academic counseling, ombudsman services, tutoring, financial aid information, job placement services, and transfer orientation. Graduates indicated that most of their friends and mentors shared the same major.

All students identified peer support as important, but support groups were most fully developed among traditional students from college-educated families. These groups provided invaluable support in many ways. Members shared the work of preparing course assignments, studying for tests, and interpreting lectures and reading materials. They advised each other about course selection, identifying the best instructors as well as those who should be avoided. Students also taught each other the basics of negotiating the bureaucracy of the university. Since such networks often included students at various stages in their programs, they provided role models and constructive competition and raised expectations of success within the system. For some, these social networks provided essential links to future opportunity.

The scaling-down process, while an essential aspect of successful adjustment for all students, was more complicated for minority students. Tendencies toward separation are aggravated by the scaling-down strategies adopted by both minority and nonminority students and by the programs colleges institute to help them. Special support programs, even if not explicitly designed for minority students, often become predominantly minority as access initiatives bring more nontraditional and underprepared minorities onto the campus.

A climate of low expectation interferes with informal student coping strategies by preventing minority students from relating to the campus environment in the same way that majority students do. While college is supposed to be an inherently broadening experience, for underrepresented minority students, attending predominantly Anglo institutions may limit access to a peer environment as well as to other aspects of the social and cognitive life of the university (Fleming, 1984). In addition, the homogeneous composition of student groups sometimes reflects underlying racism. As one Hispanic graduate said, "You have pockets, you know. Hispanics hang out together, and the whites hang out together, and the blacks hang out together. So you really don't have that interaction."

Racially and ethnically based support groups whose members come from backgrounds of severely limited opportunity sometimes exert a negative influence by reinforcing each other's low expectations for achievement and feelings of alienation from the system. The student support groups that were most effective in promoting achievement were somewhat exclusive; only those with good academic reputations were accepted. In such groups, minority students were sometimes not welcome because of stereotypes about their lack of academic motivation and skill. An older Hispanic woman graduate recalled that a fellow student in a science class had refused to be her lab partner: "This Anglo lady came over and said, 'Dr. Norton just said to choose our own group, and I really don't want you in my group. I want an A for me.' And I stood up and said, 'Look, why are you stereotyping? What makes you think I don't want an A out of this class?' That's stereotyping because they know all the statistics that you know right away; we're not aiming for an A and that's typical. . . . You're stereotyped right away. Not wanting to be on top. Of course we want to be on top."

Under such circumstances the position of minorities becomes not only separate but marginal. The concentration of minorities in special programs, within separate social networks, and in a small set of relatively low-status majors seems to justify and reinforce low expectations and the relegation of minorities to lower status. Minorities in such cases are retained without full access to the curriculum, the campus, or the chance to earn a degree (Francisco, 1983).

Institutional Strategies. Student strategies for coping with the university environment were aided by special programs and services, whether those programs were designated for minorities or for disadvantaged, underprepared, or nontraditional students. Many of our first-generation interviewees felt that they never could have made it without the support of these programs.

The most effective programs involve collaboration among universities, community colleges, and public schools to provide support for underprepared students by developing bridge programs and by providing systematic and comprehensive academic support services (such as assessment and remediation, learning laboratories, tutorial services, intrusive advising, and monitoring of student progress) until a student was firmly established in a major. The potential for success of this approach was exemplified in the experience of a Mexican American honors graduate in mechanical engineering who finished high school in the lower half of his class and was advised by a counselor to go to a vocational school. He was accepted into a summer bridge program that strengthened his academic background, clarified his educational goals, and introduced him to the academic environment. Through the program, he developed a network of friends and faculty members that provided support through five successful years.

Older adults also benefit from collaborative programs between community colleges and universities that provide opportunities to fill in gaps in preparation and that offer flexible course scheduling. Vestibule programs that provide students who fail to meet regular admissions standards with careful advising, career development, assistance in strengthening basic skills, and more personal interaction with faculty also help to scale down the campus environment.

Colleges often help students scale down along racial and ethnic lines by setting up networking groups for minority students pursuing the same major. Some institutions with relatively small populations of a particular racial or ethnic group try to provide more comfortable social environments through networking and a variety of culturally sensitive alternatives, such as special residence halls or meeting-place arrangements. At more multicultural colleges, student clubs organized according to race and ethnicity provide a sense of cultural identity and a place of refuge from the "melting pot" character of the academic environment. The graduates we interviewed recognized the vital role played by minority-focused groups. "Any incoming minority will not feel unwelcome. There is a vast number of clubs geared to specific minorities," said one Hispanic graduate. "The

National Black Students and similar clubs take it upon themselves to help minority students. I mean, we really don't rely on the school for that. If it wasn't for the NBS, my experience would be very different," a black Caribbean graduate said.

We have previously identified academic departments as especially significant in supporting students. However, admissions policies sometimes produce unequal access to academic programs. Many institutions admit students to a general program and then require the completion of specified requirements before accepting them into high-demand majors. Where the more popular programs adopt screening procedures that eliminate all but the best-prepared minority applicants, there are commonly wide fluctuations in the representation across majors. The tendency for minority students to select majors that already have significant minority participation intensifies unequal representation across departments.

Graduates reported being aware of both physical and social separation between minority and nonminority students. This occurred most at schools with smaller minority enrollments, more full-time and residential students, and a more competitive atmosphere. While others have noted that black students on white campuses prefer a degree of separation in their peer associations (Sowell, 1972; Centra, 1971), the graduates we interviewed expressed ambivalent attitudes about this apparently mutual process of separation. "You know, the campus is so big. And quite a few minorities are finding themselves in one building. Everybody socializes around this one area. I don't know how to explain this. It's feeling like you have to be around that area to fit," reported a Hispanic graduate. "The only thing that I guess was really difficult for me to understand was this segregation between blacks and whites there. You know, you had black activities and you had white activities. . . . Sometimes it made me mad, and sometimes it didn't," recalled an African American graduate.

The effectiveness of scaling-down strategies, especially when they involved a degree of racial and ethnic separation, depended on the prevailing attitudes toward minorities on campus. Too often these attitudes involved low expectations, as previously described. The importance of obtaining active faculty support for improving the climate for minority student success was apparent from the comments of graduates. "I guess the positive thing I would say would be the professors. I had a lot of good professors who took a special interest in giving me the help I needed," said one African American graduate. "Though some of the teachers are not exactly prominority, I can't really think of anything they would have changed if I had been other than a minority," reported another.

Through faculty behavior, it becomes apparent to minorities when a college wants them to succeed, although the support may be attributed to institutional self-interest. "They try to keep you there. . . . They want every freshman who comes to graduate. I don't know if that's good or bad, but they want to see you graduate, not necessarily because they like you, but . . . so more students get degrees," an African American graduate said.

While the graduates did not paint rosy pictures of utopian acceptance, most indicated that the climate of the institution attended was one in which minority students could succeed. "It was pretty much a melting pot, and everyone basically got offered the same things. I don't really think there are any particular problems that blacks have that anybody else might not have. . . . You still feel a little discrimination. It's not overt, but it's there. Those are things that you have to just overcome," said one African American graduate. "I guess there's prejudice everywhere, but I didn't find it overbearing, not enough to hurt me," said another.

Conclusion

All first-generation students are uncertain climbers. Minority students in particular need ladders with every rung in place in order to provide them with a fair opportunity for overcoming incomplete preparation, nonspecific educational objectives, and nontraditional modes of college attendance. The necessary rungs include early intervention to strengthen preparation and improve educational planning, summer bridge programs, special orientation and registration, tailored financial aid programs, assessment and remediation, tutoring, learning laboratories, mentoring, intrusive academic advising, and career development. These rungs help community colleges translate open access into a successful educational experience.

Community colleges have long viewed first-generation college-goers as a primary clientele. The importance that they attach to their teaching mission and their experience in working with underprepared majority students gives them an edge in promoting achievement among minority students with similar backgrounds. Beyond first- and second-generation minority students with differing preparations, there is a sizable pool of reasonably prepared minority adults for whom a job and family mandate a nontraditional mode of attendance.

This population is high risk. Providing them with the opportunity to achieve a degree requires close cooperation between two- and four-year colleges, as well as the assistance of a variety of state and community agencies. Offsetting the risks and difficulties of serving adults is the potential impact of their success on families and minority communities. Increasing the number of minority college graduates in traditional age groups has important long-run consequences for the social and economic viability of the nation. Increasing the number of college-educated minority parents and workers offers a short-run strategy for rekindling the American dream for people who frequently believe it has passed them by.

References

Astin, A. W. *The College Environment*. Washington, D.C.: American Council on Education, 1968.

Attinasi, L. C. "Getting In: Mexican Americans' Perception of University Attendance and the Implications for Freshman-Year Persistence." *Journal of Higher Education*, 1989, *60* (3), 247–277.

Bennett, C., and Harris, J. J. "Suspensions and Expulsions of Male and Black Students: A Case Study of the Causes of Disproportionality." *Urban Education*, 1982, *16* (4), 399–423.

Brophy, J. E., and Good, T. L. *Teacher-Student Relationship: Causes and Consequences*. New York: Holt, Rinehart & Winston, 1974.

Centra, J. A. "How Students Perceive Their College Environment." *College Board Review*, 1971, *79*, 11–13.

Dawkins, M. P., and Dawkins, R. L. "Perceptions and Experience as Correlates of Academic Performance Among Blacks at a Predominantly White University: A Research Note." *College and University*, 1980, *55* (2), 171–180.

Fleming, J. *Blacks in College: A Comparative Study of Students' Success in Black and in White Institutions*. San Francisco: Jossey-Bass, 1984.

Francisco, R. P. "Special Programs for Black Students in Higher Education: The Need for Reorganization During a Conservative Era." *Journal of Nonwhite Concerns in Personnel and Guidance*, 1983, *11* (3), 114–121.

Gilmartin, K. J. "The Status of Women and Minorities in Education: A Social Indicator Feasibility Study." *Journal of Educational Equity and Leadership*, 1980, *1* (1), 3–27.

Haynes, N. M., and Johnson, S. T. "Self- and Teacher Expectancy Effects on Academic Performance of College Students Enrolled in an Academic Reinforcement Program." *American Educational Research Journal*, 1983, *20* (4), 511–516.

Kleinbaum, D. G., and Kleinbaum, A. "The Minority Experience at a Predominantly White University: Report of a 1972 Survey at University of North Carolina at Chapel Hill." *Journal of Negro Education*, 1976, *45* (3), 312–328.

Madrazo-Peterson, R., and Rodriguez, M. "Minority Students' Perceptions of a University Environment." *Journal of College Student Personnel*, 1978, *19* (3), 259–263.

Ogbu, J. U. *Minority Education and Caste: The American System in Cross-Cultural Perspective*. San Diego, Calif.: Academic Press, 1978.

Ogbu, J. U. "Variability in Minority School Performance: A Problem in Search of an Explanation." *Anthropology and Education Quarterly*, 1987, *18* (4), 312–334.

Oliver, M. L., Rodriguez, C. J., and Mickelson, R. A. "Brown and Black in White: The Social Adjustment and Academic Performance of Chicano and Black Students in a Predominantly White University." *Urban Review*, 1985, *17* (1), 3–24.

Richardson, R. C., Jr., Fisk, E. C., and Okun, M. A. *Literacy in the Open-Access College*. San Francisco: Jossey-Bass, 1983.

Richardson, R. C., Jr., and Skinner, E. F. *Achieving Quality and Diversity: Universities in a Multicultural Society*. New York: Macmillan, 1991.

Rist, R. C. "Student Social Class and Teacher Expectation: The Self-Fulfilling Prophecy in Ghetto Education." *Harvard Educational Review*, 1970, *40* (3), 411–445.

St. John, N. H. *School Desegregation: Outcomes for Children*. New York: Wiley, 1975.

Skinner, E. F., and Richardson, R. C., Jr. "Making It in a Majority University: The Minority Graduate's Perspective." *Change*, 1988, *20* (3), 34–42.

Sowell, T. *Black Education: Myths and Tragedies*. New York: McKay, 1972.

Suen, H. K. "Alienation and Attrition of Black College Students on a Predominantly White Campus." *Journal of College Student Personnel*, 1983, *24* (12), 117–121.

Tinto, V. *Leaving College: Rethinking the Causes and Cures of Student Attrition*. Chicago: University of Chicago Press, 1987.

Tracey, T. J., and Sedlacek, W. E. "Prediction of College Graduation Using Noncognitive Variables by Race." *Measurement and Evaluation in Counseling and Development,* 1987, *19* (4), 177–184.

U.S. Civil Rights Commission. *Teachers and Students—Report 5: Mexican American Education Study—Differences in Teacher Interaction with Mexican American and Anglo Students.* Washington, D.C.: U.S. Civil Rights Commission, 1973.

Western Interstate Commission for Higher Education. *The Ecosystem Model: Designing the Campus Environment.* Boulder, Colo.: Western Interstate Commission for Higher Education, 1973

Wheelis, T. J. *The Classroom Environment: Developing a Holistic Approach to Minority Student Retention.* Paper presented at the New Mexico Personnel and Guidance Association Annual Conference Workshop, Albuquerque, April 1982.

RICHARD C. RICHARDSON, JR., is associate director of the National Center for Postsecondary Governance at Arizona State University.

ELIZABETH FISK SKINNER is a faculty member in arts and sciences at Gateway Community College, Phoenix, Arizona.

Adult first-generation students, like younger first-generation students, must confront cultural issues, but unlike their younger cohorts, these adults have established independent lives, which complicates their transition to college life.

First-Generation Adult Students: In Search of Safe Havens

L. Steven Zwerling

To someone of my generation who began college teaching during the 1960s, the typical student one encountered was the "traditional age," from eighteen to twenty-two. True, there were any number of "nontraditional" students on campus, especially if you were on the faculty of a community college; such students included returning Vietnam veterans, women whose children were old enough to allow them to begin or continue their college education ("returning women"), dislocated workers seeking retraining, and so on. But the predominant campus climate was shaped by the values and life-styles of the young people who were its primary citizens.

As a youthful faculty member, younger than thirty and therefore presumably still trustworthy, I felt part of the culture that was then so widely reported, a culture that among other things questioned all authority, including that of my college, along with its curriculum and its methods. Thus, when a number of the more "progressive" faculty became concerned about the many seemingly able students who stopped attending after a semester or two, we chose not to join the grousing sessions in the faculty cafeteria that assigned all blame to the students but instead began to search for the institutional factors that might be contributing to this terrible attrition.

My Reeducation

Frankly, I needed to be reeducated. My formal training was in English and comparative literature. I knew nothing about education itself—nothing about the history of schooling, about curriculum (except the local politics of how to get a new course approved), or about what some were calling the "hidden curriculum" or social functions of education. A quick immersion in the literature of schooling, especially that of the critics—Katz (1968), Karabel (1972), Greer (1972), Aronowitz (1973), and Freire (1971)—led my colleagues and me to sense that in spite of the egalitarian rhetoric and open-door policy of community colleges, they provided more the illusion of opportunity than the reality. As I began to dig deeper into the writings about community colleges while I was working on my book, *Second Best: The Crisis of the Community College* (1976), and particularly as I read the primary historical documents, including the early state master plans for higher education in California and elsewhere, it became clear to me that community colleges had come into being as much to divert students away from senior institutions, so that they could maintain selective admissions practices, as to provide second-chance opportunities for the academically less successful. I also came on an early work by Burton Clark (1960) that saw the primary role for the junior college to be the "cooling out" of students—that is, through counseling, to convince the less successful that their lack of achievement was their own and not the institution's fault. This struck an all-too-familiar note: what Clark described reminded me of practices I had long encountered on my own campus. From students, I had heard many stories, similar to the one Julia Lara recounts in this volume, of counselors and faculty members who had tried to get students to be "realistic," to lower their aspirations at the first sign of academic difficulty. Recognizing this pattern ultimately led my colleagues and me to change our ways of working with students—to attempt, instead, to "heat them up," to help them discover their true potential, and to maintain or raise their aspirations. All this is described in detail in *Second Best*.

By 1976, then, my colleagues and I, as well as others in community colleges around the country, were finding ways to work more effectively with the rather small numbers of students we encountered. Nevertheless, the national data on the academic progress of two-year college students indicated that a shrinking proportion of at-risk students were succeeding. As one measure of this, the transfer rate of low-income and minority students who were more and more found in community colleges continued to decline. In California, for example, where nearly 90 percent of minority students enrolled in college were found at community colleges, only 5 to 10 percent transferred, less than half the rate of white students. One clearly needed to look beyond the master plans and cooling-out practices to seek reasons for this institutional ineffectiveness.

My own reading took me next to the work of Howard London (1978), Lois Weis (1985), and Richard Richardson with Elizabeth Fisk and Morris Okun (1983). In different ways, each wrote about how the institutional culture of the community college must be considered when thinking about how to work with at-risk students. London and Weis showed how first-generation students from working-class backgrounds, in order to be successful, to achieve aspirations that might take them away from their families and neighborhoods, needed to function in two worlds simultaneously—that of their parents and friends and that of the more cosmopolitan, middle-class college. Thus, ironically and sadly, success usually required a renegotiation of relationships with family and friends as students began to see themselves differently; failure was often more ascribable to an unwillingness to undertake this renegotiation than to any fundamental lack of ability or diligence.

Richardson, Fisk, and Okun's (1983) examination of the academic culture of the community college revealed, in addition, that between a demoralized faculty and students whose primary goal was to acquire basic information, there existed a silent agreement to lower intellectual demands so that neither instructors nor students would be taxed. This "leveled-down" or remedialized environment, which valued rote learning more than analytical or critical thinking, enabled students to pursue the vocational goals that had become dominant on two-year college campuses, while allowing the faculty to teach out their remaining years in relative comfort. Such a debased academic climate, however, greatly thwarted the chances of those students with higher academic aspirations—how could they receive the preparation they needed in order to transfer to a senior college? Richardson, Fisk, and Okun mused that this culture of lowered expectations might well contribute to the declining fortunes of community college transfer students.

It was obvious to those of us who encountered this new literature that we would have to address these cultural issues directly, that in our counseling and advisement we would need to help first-generation students find ways to build bridges between the worlds they were required to negotiate, and that in our work with faculty we would need to get them to grapple with ways to enrich the academic climate. None of this seemed simple to achieve, though a number of successful efforts of this kind are described in later chapters.

Adult Students: The New Majority

Also at about this time, it became clear that the familiar traditional student was no longer in the majority, that the "nontraditional" adult, part-time student with work and family responsibilities was more commonly found on community college campuses. Indeed, few of the old descriptions of two-year colleges and their students pertained: it was no longer possible to separate the traditional functions as neatly as it had been in the past into collegiate, career, compensatory, and community divisions. How could one classify an adult who attended intermittently, initially taking skills courses and then credit courses in business, who got an associate in applied science degree in computer technology, and eventually transferred to a four-year college? In effect, this student fit into all four categories. How many students were actually taking two years to complete the two-year college? How many transfer students were actually transferring? How many terminal students were terminating? Indeed, evidence was accumulating that more vocational students were transferring than academic students. Why on many campuses were there more reverse transfers than forward transfers?

In this new community college, one thing remained unchanged: for those students with aspirations that included the eventual attainment of a bachelor's degree, the likelihood that this would occur was still bleak. In fact, although there are few sets of meaningful data that compare the academic success rates of adults with traditional-age students, the available information does indicate that part-time students, not surprisingly, fare considerably less well than full-time students. If one wishes to discover the causes for this lack of academic progress, all of the familiar reasons pertain, with one exception: the cultural tensions that complicate the lives of first-generation college-age students are quite different from those that play on adults.

Most of the cultural literature concerns itself with younger students—for example, in their fieldwork, London (1978) and Weis (1985) have generally studied the lives of traditional-age students who are the first in their families to go to college. Little is said about first-generation students who attend while working and raising families. From what can be gleaned from the literature and from the interviews I conducted with adult students in preparation for writing this chapter, there are inklings of significant differences that educators need to consider as they seek ways to help more of these students fulfill their aspirations.

For younger first-generation college students, as we have seen, seeking upward mobility usually involves risking the disapproval of family and friends who see college attendance itself and the resulting taking on of new values and modes of behavior as a form of disloyalty. In London's words in Chapter One, such conflicts "inevitably call into question the very meaning of allegiance and love."

For adult first-generation students who have already moved out of their parents' home, have been working full time, perhaps have begun a family of their own, and have come under the influence of educated role models in the world of work—in other words, for those who are now the more typical community college student—the direct cultural pressures that younger students feel on virtually a daily basis are greatly diminished. Indeed, in the literature and from my interviews, there is evidence that rather than experiencing a pull back toward the world of the old neighborhood, adult students are frequently encouraged to pursue a higher education by their new friends at work, by their supervisors, and by their own children and spouses.

Let me now present brief portraits of two adult students who exemplify this new reality as a way of furthering our understanding of their lives and aspirations. In both cases, I have changed the students' names and some of the facts of their lives in order to preserve their anonymity.

Cynthia Brown. Cynthia Brown was born in Harlem forty years ago. Her mother died when she was quite young, and she was raised, along with her two brothers, by her father. She is the youngest child, and in her view, little was expected of her. Though she did well in elementary and high school, all her father envisioned for her was that she get a job. Nor did she receive any encouragement to pursue her education from her teachers or friends. No one in the neighborhood was college bound, and Cynthia never gave college a thought. She felt fortunate when she was able to find a clerk's job at a bank after she graduated; she was, in fact, the first in her immediate family to finish high school.

The years moved along quickly. She did well at work, adding work friends to those from the neighborhood where she continued to live in an apartment of her own. When she was twenty-seven, she had a son who brought her great joy. Her father and brothers remained close by, as did her nieces and nephews. Cynthia lived in the midst of a loving extended family and considered herself blessed as she saw many with whom she had grown up drift into frustration and despair.

But as her son grew older, inevitably turning to friends for basic companionship, Cynthia found herself with more time to think about her own fortunes. At work, though she advanced somewhat and was beginning to make "good money," she saw others with more formal education, people she had "broken in" when they were hired, move past her into the better positions. Thus, about five years ago, entirely on her own, Cynthia began to consider college. "I began to think that I wanted to make something else of my life. Frankly, I wanted to be in a position to get promoted, to make more money, maybe be able to get a better job at another bank, even though I was happy where I was. I realized that a college degree on the résumé was what I needed."

As many people at the bank assumed she already had been to college, she was initially embarrassed to discuss her emerging plans with anyone there. Two of her nieces, however, had gone to college, and she felt comfortable talking with them. They were very encouraging. Still, she was reluctant to bring the idea up with either her father or brothers, even though if she decided to "take the plunge," she would have to call on them to sit with her son an evening or two a week when she was in class. She is not sure even today, when she reflects back, why she could not bring herself to raise this issue with her immediate family; perhaps it was the residue of feeling not encouraged when she was younger. She did, though, eventually find a way to open the subject and at the same time to test herself: she enrolled in a computer training course in a trade school. Although it was not discussed at the time, she believed that her father and brothers approved, as it was an appropriate thing for her to do, given the nature of her job and her abilities. It would also allow her to see if she could manage working and going to school at the same time.

She exceeded her expectations and, as a result, began to broach the subject of applying to college both with her family and her supervisor at work. She was surprised to find them all supportive. For the first time in her life, her father told her he was proud of her, and her supervisor indicated that he had all along thought of her as "college material" and that if she completed an associate degree in a business-related subject, he would arrange for her to be promoted.

And enroll Cynthia did. Quickly, however, there were problems at home, in the office, and in the neighborhood. Of greatest concern was the reaction of her son, now thirteen. He was the least supportive of her family. "His attitude changed. He didn't tell me directly, but there was an air of tension in the house. I think he was a little jealous of all the time I was spending in class and with my homework. I wished that he had understood that I was doing it in part for him, that I was trying to set an example by going to college, by doing all the reading I was required to do. In the past all I ever read were magazines. I was hoping that some of it would rub off on him. So far I haven't seen much change, but I have to keep at it because I have to have my life even if it makes my son a little unhappy."

Among her friends in the office and among her high school friends in the neighborhood, Cynthia began to feel estranged. She sensed that she was changing, especially as the result of her reading, and some of them clearly resented it. She was moving beyond them. She longed to be able to discuss what she was discovering, but when she tried, it didn't work: "I wanted to talk about my reading, but they turned away, and now it hurts to say it but I find myself losing interest in them." There were a few friends who had gone to college, two at work particularly, to whom Cynthia grew closer and who provided a continuous stream of encouragement. "My supervisor, too, is keeping an eye on how I'm doing and keeps telling me that as the result of some early retirements there may be room for me to move up."

For Cynthia and for many women of her background and generation, it was not unusual as a youngster not to be encouraged to go to college or to think about a career, and it was not unusual for Cynthia and for others like her not to break away from the expectations of their families or the larger culture in which they grew up. There were too many boundaries to cross, too many people to confront even to contemplate a different path. As with so many, she needed to find and test herself later in life in the world outside her family and neighborhood before she could even say to her peers that she wanted something different. Unlike her younger colleagues at college, Cynthia, as an adult, as someone who had established a life that bridged the two worlds that defined her, was able to redefine herself and find ways to explain herself to family and friends, in the end receiving their encouragement and support.

Selma Rodriguez. Selma Rodriguez was born in Puerto Rico forty-two years ago, the sixth of seven children. When she was a toddler, the family moved to New York City, settling in the South Bronx. As Selma says, it wasn't called the South Bronx at that time but was nearly as bad then as it was "discovered" to be two decades later. Neither of her parents completed elementary school, and it was years before they were able to engage in even a basic conversation in English. As the second youngest, Selma was fortunate when it came time for her to begin school; her parents were doing a little better, and they were able to afford the tuition to send her to parochial school. She fared reasonably well and was able to continue in Catholic high school, but she didn't score high enough on the admissions test to be placed on the academic track as her English skills were not yet well enough developed. Instead, she found herself, along with all the other Hispanic students, in the commercial program. Depending on how well one did, it was possible to switch onto the academic track; although Selma was perhaps doing well enough, she had neither the inclination nor did she receive the encouragement from family or teachers to think about it. In fact, with the exception of her second-year English teacher, not one of her other teachers ever did more than give her grades—no one passed along comments or suggestions about how she might do better work.

Things were not much different at home or in the neighborhood. None of her friends or relatives even thought about college. "It wasn't something that was discussed. Also, being female at that time, we weren't encouraged to excel in school. Most of the girls in my family got married right out of high school.

"Actually, you didn't even expect to work. You were just to stay home. You did know there was something better out there—to earn enough money to be able to move to a better neighborhood."

Selma, however, did not get married until later, and out of necessity she went to work. This was not new for her; she had been working part time since she was fifteen. After three years as a secretary in a brokerage house, she got married. Her husband was in the air force and was sent to South Carolina. There she immediately got pregnant and gave birth to the first of her two children. About two years later, they moved back to New York City. Her husband had left the service, and Selma stayed home for the next three years, raising the children while her husband went to college on the GI bill.

When the children were a little older and her husband had completed his degree, Selma went back to work as a teacher's assistant at a nearby child-care center. This got her thinking about the possibility of college for herself. "I loved working with the children and enjoyed the idea of having that title, 'teacher.' I thought it would be a goal to accomplish. I talked with the teacher I worked with, and she was very encouraging. I remember her saying, 'You can do it.' I hadn't ever thought about it. The only time anyone had encouraged me was years ago during high school when I had an interest in drawing. I'd show something to my father and *he never discouraged me not to continue*" (emphasis added).

Selma's husband also offered encouragement and agreed to take on additional responsibilities at home so that she could attend classes and do homework. By now most of her immediate family had either returned to Puerto Rico or scattered to other states. Only her youngest brother and one of her sisters remained in the area, and they were both supportive. Indeed, a number of years after Selma had begun college, they both started taking courses, she believes, largely as a result of her experiences. Her children, too, provided essential assistance, never once making her feel guilty that she was less available to them. Indeed, as the years of Selma's schooling stretched out, both her children entered college and her husband returned to school to work on his master's. She recalls many evenings when all four of them sat around the kitchen table studying together.

But college was difficult for her. Though she did well, managing to get on the dean's list a couple of times, and though she has completed an associate degree and is ten credits shy of her bachelor's in communications, Selma is and always has been "petrified" every time she goes to a class. "I don't understand it. It must somehow be rooted in me that I can't do well. Even when I get a good grade I find reasons to explain it away—either the course was easy or the instructor took pity on me. I would love to find a way to get some kind of assurance that it's because of me."

Some of her old friends from high school days are ambivalent about her success. One in particular keeps asking, "Aren't you tired? Are you sure you want to do this?" Selma senses that this friend really doesn't want her to continue, that she fears she will lose her. "I tell her, 'I want to do it. I have to do it.' "

She also realizes now, many years later, that she was by no means solely responsible for not thinking about or pursuing a college education earlier. She sees "outside forces" to be the primary deterrent. "From some of my classes and from the reading I've done, I think little was expected of me because I'm a woman and Hispanic. It's not that I felt prejudice directly; it's more that that's the way things were. I had to figure out how to make my own way."

Like Cynthia Brown, Selma Rodriguez indeed needed to make her own way. She, too, needed to establish a world apart as a base from which to begin to view herself in new ways. From this safe haven she was able to consider new possibilities for herself, allowing herself to come under the influence of adults who had created lives for themselves that were different from any she had witnessed at home or in the neighborhood. But it was not entirely without cost. Though she received essential support from her husband and children, she was clearly in the process of being estranged from the last of her childhood friends. And as she crossed irrevocably into the world of the educated, she remained riddled by self-doubt and uncertain about the meaning of her accomplishments. She is, though, committed to continuing the process, acknowledging that she now knows how much more she needs and wants to know and how sheltered she used to be.

Working with Adult Students

If first-generation adult students appear to be able to function in two worlds more effectively than younger students do, why then do so many still not complete their studies? And what can we do to help more of them succeed? There are at least three things we can do as educators, based on our understanding of their realities: first, we should reexamine some of our assumptions about what constitutes a meaningful curriculum; second, we should take another look at the appropriateness of some of our teaching methods; and third, we would be wise to reconsider some of the ways in which we advise and counsel our adult students.

As part-time, intermittent students, adults experience the curriculum disjointedly, taking periodic courses, stopping in and out of school, some terms enrolling in one course and others in two or three. At most community colleges where the general education component of the curriculum tends to lack a superstructure, where course substitutions and "guided electives" are everywhere allowed, and where advanced courses are rarely offered, it is virtually impossible to get a coherent education. As adult students are more likely than their more youthful counterparts to be seeking a coherent education as part of their search for meaning in their lives (as well as for degrees and training), many give up in frustration when coherence seems impossible to attain. We should, therefore, explore ways to organize general education requirements, at least, into coherent clusters of interdisciplinary courses that center around themes and that can stand alone as well as cohere. We should also consider offering them in "executive" formats—that is, in efficiently organized blocks of time so that time-pressured adults can fit them into their lives. Two good examples of this kind of approach can be found in Miami-Dade's core curriculum and the EXCEL program at Fordham University.

Next, we should reexamine our teaching methods. If as Richardson, Fisk, and Okun (1983) found and as I discussed earlier, the academic environment of many community colleges has been leveled down, if instructors are teaching for and rewarding rote learning, adults who enroll in large part to search for meaning and redefinition will be driven away in frustration. Thus, particularly for our adult students who enroll for generative rather than instrumental reasons, we need a pedagogy that emphasizes critical and analytical thinking, a methodology that values the pursuit of understanding, not just information and skills.

Finally, we need to seek more appropriate ways to advise and counsel adult students, especially those who are the first in their families to go to college. To do this, we need to know more about the journeys already undertaken by the Cynthia Browns and Selma Rodriguezes—where they come from, the worlds they have negotiated, the distances they still have to traverse. Here I am attracted to Jack Mezirow's (1978) notion of perspective transformation, a process through which adults, preferably with our assistance, explore the meaning of their personal histories and discover that if they do not exert some effort, they may find themselves trapped in those histories, destined to live them to conclusions not of their own devising. It should be encouraging to us that the adult students we are likely to meet are already far along in this process; they would not have returned to school otherwise. We merely encounter them at a certain point in their journey. Our job, I believe, is to validate what they have accomplished thus far, encourage them to continue, and reach out actively to them if they falter.

References

Aronowitz, S. *False Promises: The Shaping of American Working-Class Consciousness.* New York: McGraw-Hill, 1973.

Clark, B. R. *The Open-Door College: A Case Study.* New York: McGraw-Hill, 1960.

Freire, P. *Pedagogy of the Oppressed.* New York: Seabury Press, 1971.

Greer, C. *The Great School Legend: A Revisionist Interpretation of American Public Education.* New York: Basic Books, 1972.

Karabel, J. "Community Colleges and Social Stratification." *Harvard Educational Review,* 1972, 42 (4), 521–562.

Katz, M. *The Irony of Early School Reform: Educational Innovation in Mid-19th Century Massachusetts.* Cambridge, Mass.: Harvard University Press, 1968.

London, H. B. *The Culture of a Community College.* New York: Praeger, 1978.

Mezirow, J. "Education for Perspective Transformation: Women's Reentry Programs in Community Colleges." New York: Center for Adult Education, Columbia University, 1978. 63 pp. (ED 166 367)

Richardson, R. C., Jr., Fisk, E. C., and Okun, M. A. *Literacy in the Open-Access College.* San Francisco: Jossey-Bass, 1983.

Weis, L. *Between Two Worlds: Black Students in an Urban Community College.* New York: Routledge & Kegan Paul, 1985.

Zwerling, L. S. *Second Best: The Crisis of the Community College.* New York: McGraw-Hill, 1976.

L. Steven Zwerling is program officer for the community college program at the Ford Foundation.

People of color are often changed by higher education, but now institutions themselves must change in order to accommodate culturally diverse student populations.

From the Barrio to the Academy: Revelations of a Mexican American "Scholarship Girl"

Laura I. Rendón

It was during my first year of graduate school at the University of Michigan, far away from the Laredo, Texas, barrio where I spent my youth, that I read Richard Rodriguez's (1975) poignant essay, "Going Home Again: The New American Scholarship Boy." Reading this story of how the academy changes foreigners who enter its culture (more than it is changed by them) inspired a powerful emotional response in me. My own odyssey through higher education had taken me along an unusual path—from a community college to one of the nation's most prestigious research universities. Engaged in Rodriguez's revealing thoughts and feelings in a dark library reading room, which I presumed to be much like the British Museum where Rodriguez had worked on his dissertation, I, too, began to experience, although not quite fully understand, the pain that comes from cultural separation. I began to think about how the rewards of academic success were in stark conflict with most of my past. And I began to empathize with the portrait that Rodriguez had read about in Richard Hoggart's (1970) *Uses of Literacy*—the image of a scholarship boy who can attain academic success only if he replaces allegiance to his native culture with loyalty to a new academic culture. "In the end . . . he must choose between the two worlds: if he intends to succeed as a student, he must, literally and figuratively, separate himself from his family, with its gregarious life, and find a quiet place to be alone with his thoughts. . . . For the loss he might otherwise feel, the scholarship boy substitutes an enormous enthusiasm for nearly everything having to do with school" (Rodriguez, 1975, p. 17).

NEW DIRECTIONS FOR COMMUNITY COLLEGES, no. 80, Winter 1992   © Jossey-Bass Publishers

To become an academic success, Rodriguez, too, had learned that he must sever his ties with the past. For example, he discovered that he had to forget the Spanish language in favor of English. He began to believe that assimilation into the mainstream culture was the key to total success. He described the regrets his parents had about how education had changed him and had "put big ideas into his head." He recounted the anguish of feeling uncomfortable with his parents when he went home with his newfound identity. What had been intimate conversations now became polite interviews.

The parallels between Rodriguez and me were obvious. Both of us had Mexican American parents who wanted their children to have a better life than they did. Our parents had never acquired a firm command of the English language but understood that learning English was essential for social advancement. Nonetheless, my parents did not understand what higher education could offer (or even take away), as they had only received a second- and third-grade education. Both Rodriguez and I were unique within our families. Rodriguez had conducted research to obtain a Ph.D. in English Renaissance literature, and I was working on a doctorate in higher education administration. As the first in my family to take this long journey into the mystifying world of higher education, I asked myself, if Rodriguez was the new American "scholarship boy," was I the new American "scholarship girl"? Did I really need to reject my past in order to attain success in the present? Was there some way in which to reconcile days gone by with my contemporary experiences?

For the young scholar who first experiences academic shock—a feeling of alienation that moves the student from concrete to abstract experience and that takes the student from an old culture that is vastly different in tradition, style, and values to a new world of unfamiliar intellectual conventions, practices, and assumptions—these questions are not easily answered. I did not know at the time that the barometer the academy uses to differentiate the academic elite from the mediocre is precisely the measure of how well young scholars negotiate academic shock. If the student, like Rodriguez, silences the past and humbly waits to be confirmed into the community of scholars, the academy swiftly offers its greatest rewards. If the student persists in using past experience to affirm himself or herself, not only do rewards become more difficult to attain but the student is also riddled with the guilt, pain, and confusion that arise from daring to live simultaneously in two vastly different worlds while being fully accepted in neither.

My Own Journey

My early beginnings are in stark contrast with my present. Recently, as I was being recruited for a faculty position at a southwestern university, I was told that I was one of the most marketable Hispanic females in the field of higher education. I sometimes wonder how I merit such praise. My trip from the barrio to the academy has hardly been silky smooth. I still remember the first time I actually made a decision to attend college. I was thirteen and in the eighth grade when a counselor came to my English class and announced that on that day we had to make a decision about whether we were going to be on the academic or the vocational track. When I asked the counselor to explain the difference, she forthrightly explained that the academic track was for those who were going to college and that the vocational track was for those who planned to get a job after high school graduation. I had always dreamed of being a teacher, so the choice was an easy one for me. I remember going home that afternoon and proudly telling my mother of my decision. Her response triggered the first painful feelings of academic shock. Dismayed and frustrated, she said, *"Estás loca. Como piensas ir al colegio si nadie de nuestra familia ha ido? Eso es para los ricos."* (You're crazy. How can you think of going to college if no one in the family has? That is for the rich.) For my mother, the choice would have been clear. In our family going to college was not an option; it never had been and it never would be. Higher education belonged to the elite, the wealthy, and we clearly were not in that group.

My pain and disappointment did not, however, interrupt my plans. I persisted in following my dream, and on graduating from high school I promptly enrolled in my local community college. Little did I know then that despite its self-proclaimed magnanimous goal of being a "people's college," the community college has also served to ghettoize people of color. In general, Hispanics, Native Americans, and African Americans tend to enroll in community colleges as opposed to four-year institutions. People like me, whom Madrid (1990) describes as *flor de tierra* (plants whose roots do not go deep), are not likely to enter higher education through the front door. We do not apply to wealthy liberal arts colleges or to institutions whose prestige is unquestioned. With Madrid, I believe that most students like me enter higher education through its windows, only to find that all around us are walls that keep us secluded and marginalized. Nonetheless, Laredo Junior College became for me the first access point to the world of higher education.

At Laredo Junior College I found both the comforts and discomforts of attending college with my friends; we were not only uncertain about our future but perplexed about what it would take to succeed in this new world of higher education. It was here, in this illusory intellectual oasis of the Laredo community, that I experienced some of the sensations of academic shock, as I faced new academic demands and tried to reconcile my new world with my old culture. I knew that my mother was feeling angry and frustrated with my tenacious desire to go to college, although we never really talked about it. It was a subject that was broached in different ways.

She would explain that she was tired of being a waitress. She would be irritable that she had to work night shifts in order to sustain the family (my two sisters and me). I knew that for her the ideal daughter would promptly, after graduating from high school, get a job so that her mother would not have to work anymore. Even today I often find myself trying to make up for the fact that I did not fit this ideal vision.

My friends at Laredo Junior College not only shared my family's experience of economic hardship but they also seemed lost in this new world of abstraction. Suddenly, our professors expected us, with no guidance, to have clarity about our vague dreams and goals, to express ourselves in rational, analytic forms, and to put aside our personal anxieties and frustrations so that we could be successful college students.

The few of us who tried to transfer to an institution away from home experienced the pain and conflict of academic shock even more acutely. My parents told me that if I must transfer, I should go to a nearby institution. I felt, however, that I needed to get further away, to experience something dramatically different. The pull of the academy was overwhelming. During my sophomore year, due to poor counseling, I found both that it was too late to apply to a four-year institution and that my local community college was not offering any more courses in my program of study (English and journalism education). Feeling the need to stay on track and continue my studies, I transferred to San Antonio College. It was here, 150 miles away from home, that I first experienced the loneliness that often overcomes scholarship boys and girls. In this community college, I felt isolated and disconnected. None of my professors were minority, and the other Mexican American students also seemed lost and alienated. I felt that my white professors did not recognize my academic potential. None made any special effort to encourage me to perform at my best. In San Antonio, I not only felt alienated from my family but I found myself being perceived differently by them. Living away from home was, indeed, changing me. To cope, I found comfort in reading, and I was especially intrigued by what I read for my philosophy class. Yet I never talked about Sartre or Plato with any of my family members. These new ideas seemed to belong only within the confines of the collegiate environment. Subconsciously, I must have felt that the language of college did not belong in my family life. The two were separate and incompatible. Reflecting on new learning while at the same time coping with the feeling of not belonging made me more introverted.

When I transferred again to the University of Houston, the pain of separation became even greater. My mother, wanting to be certain that I was living in a safe place, took the long bus trip with me to Houston. She wept when I told her that I had gotten a grant, that I had a dormitory room, and that everything would be all right. It was in Houston that I came face to face with being a minority. Academic shock was compounded by ethnic and racial shock. In Laredo, a community of over 90 percent Mexican Americans, we were all the same, but here I was keenly aware of being different. At the University of Houston in 1968, during the thick of racial and social unrest, there were few Mexican American or black students. I met no Mexican American professors, and there was only one black faculty member who taught journalism on a part-time basis. My dorm roommates were white, but despite our differences, we learned from each other and became good friends. Coping with academic life was difficult and exacerbated by my separation from my family and culture. When I would call my mother and explain how busy I was, she would encourage me to come home and give up everything. *"Vente, hija"* (Come back daughter), she would say, *"ya deja todo eso"* (and leave everything behind). It was her motherly duty to protect her child from the unknown.

When I graduated from college, I wanted to stay and teach in Houston, but my parents insisted I return to Laredo. "You have much education," my father explained, "but you lack experience," emphasizing that experience was necessary for coping with real life. Once I asked my mother why she resisted my leaving home to be by myself. *"Tengo miedo, hija"* (I am afraid, daughter), she would say. When I asked her what she was afraid of, she simply responded, *"No sé"* (I don't know). I sensed that deep in my mother's soul she felt resentful about how this alien culture of higher education was polluting my values and customs. I, in turn, was afraid that I was becoming a stranger to her, a stranger she did not quite understand, a stranger she might not even like.

Connections with the Past

Today, I am asked to speak to educators about people like me, people of color who come to the academy as strangers in a strange land. And often what intrigues them most is not what I have to say about how education can best serve these students but how my own journey progressed. "How did you succeed?" they ask. "If you succeeded, why can't others?" While these questions are often asked out of genuine curiosity and concern, I sometimes become irritated because they seem to me to be tied to the belief that if only students like me were not lazy, if only they would shed their past, if only they would be truly loyal and dedicated to schooling, they, too, could succeed. "Pure" academics who subscribe to Euro-centered rationalism and objectivity do not wish to read personal, emotional, or intuitive essays like mine that focus on the past. To them, these recollections are, at best, primitive and self-serving and, at worst, romanticized nonsense. True scholarship "boys and girls" would focus on objective modes of expression, on the present and future, and if the past must be recalled, it must be only as something that should be left behind or neatly put away. To succeed we must assimilate, become one of "them," and learn what Rodriguez (1975) calls "the great lesson of school"—that in order to have a public identity, we must use only English, for if Spanish or other foreign languages are employed, feelings of public separateness will be reinforced. The academy is set up so that students most likely to succeed are those that can successfully disconnect from the past and turn over their loyalty to the conventions and practices of the academy. Yet, academic success can be attained without total disconnection, and many educators either do not want to accept this or fail to recognize this.

Certainly there are many times now when I feel alienated from the world from which I came. What keeps me separate are my education, where I live, who my new friends are, my career, my values, and my command of the English language. For seven years I lived away from the Southwest. When I lived in Virginia, South Carolina, and North Carolina, I was invariably asked what a person like me was doing, living in the South away from my culture. But I have never been totally separate, and I never really will be or want to be. Leaving Texas led to a deeper appreciation of the world from which I came, to an enhanced understanding of other cultural values and ideologies, and to a stronger commitment to conducting research that could help two- and four-year colleges enhance the educational experience of students of color. I have learned that the past is always with me. What connects me to my past is what gives me my identity—my command of the Spanish language, the focus of my research, my old friends, and my heritage. What makes Laura Rendón an individual is not only who she is now but what happened to her along the way. What gives me strength is my newfound ability to trust and follow my own natural style and to encourage others to do the same.

Lessons to Be Learned

What is to be learned from a Mexican American scholarship girl/woman who felt intense pressure to assimilate into the academy and who is now a university professor who publishes in juried journals, attends meetings comprised predominantly of white males, and addresses predominantly white audiences? I contend that the most important lesson to be learned is *not* that higher education must increase access for new scholarship "boys and girls" or must offer them better financial aid packages, more role models, and better counseling and mentoring. These standard solutions, while important, do not focus on the larger and more important issue, which is that higher education must begin to think in new ways about what constitutes intellectual development and about whether the traditional manner with which education prepares new students is appropriate for people of color as well as for white women and men. The model that higher education now follows is based on what the authors of *Women's Ways of Knowing* (Belenky, Clinchy, Goldberger, and Tarule, 1986) describe as the "masculine myth." In this model, the scholarship boy/man is admitted into the fraternity of powerful knowers only when he has learned to think in complex, abstract ways, when he has learned to recognize that past experience is a source not of strength but of error. Once certified as a thinker who thinks like "them," students have learned that doubt precedes belief. The great lesson learned is that separation leads to academic power.

This paradigm validates the portrait of the "scholarship boy" with which Richard Rodriguez identified. If this model most appropriately describes the course of male intellectual development, where confirmation to a community of scholars is calculated to occur only at the end of a program of study, then so be it. But I believe this model is not appropriate for women or for people of color. For us, it is important that from the beginning of our college career, our professors express their sincere belief that we are capable of learning and can be taught to learn. Often we enter higher education consumed with self-doubt. We doubt our intellectual capacity; we question whether we really belong in the academy; we doubt whether our research interests are really valid. This doubt is reinforced by the subtle yet powerful messages that higher education institutions communicate. For example, we hear loud and clear that only white men can do science and math, that only the best and the brightest deserve to be educated, that white students are inherently smarter than nonwhites, and that allowing people of color to enter a college diminishes its academic quality.

When I entered the University of Michigan, I remember being overwhelmed by its intellectual ethos. I recall listening to my white graduate student counterparts talk about their undergraduate experiences in liberal arts colleges and prestigious universities that appeared to be of higher quality than the institutions I had attended. I wondered whether I could compete with these students whose experiences were so different from my own. One white woman graduate student actually found the courage to reveal her stereotyped views of Hispanics and said, "You know, Laura, you're pretty smart. I'll have to admit that when I first met you, I thought you were kind of dumb." Higher education often requires not only that students be humble but that they tolerate humiliation. I remember wanting to study Chicanos in community colleges and wondering if the focus of my research would typecast me as a unidimensional (and therefore less worthy) scholar, capable of studying, writing, and thinking only about minority issues. I also wondered why, even when I had penetrated the walls of an esteemed university, I continued to focus my research on community colleges. I remember one of my friends telling me, "Why are you studying community colleges? I mean, community colleges—who cares?" He did not understand that I cared because community colleges were where people like me were gaining access to higher education, and because, unlike me, many of these people entered college, got nowhere, and left.

Nonetheless, I asked myself why I wasn't breaking away from this niche and studying other kinds of institutions.

My story's lesson is that it is not only students who must adapt to a new culture but institutions that must allow themselves to be changed by foreign cultures. A few years ago, I read Galarza's (1970) perspective on institutional deviancy. Institutions become deviant, he explained, when they inflict pain on individuals, when they begin to depart from their moral and statutory commitment. There is no doubt in my mind that higher education has inflicted great pain on students of color.

To become academic success stories we must endure humiliation, reject old values and traditions, mistrust our experience, and disconnect with our past. Ironically, the academy preaches freedom of thought and expression but demands submission and loyalty. Scholarship "boys and girls" are left only with what Rodriguez (1982) calls "hunger of memory," a nostalgic longing for the past—the laughter of relatives, the beautiful intimacy of the Spanish language, the feeling of closeness with one's own parents.

How can institutions change? It is my belief that institutions must consider past experience, language, and culture as strengths to be respected and woven into the fabric of knowledge production and dissemination, not as deficits that must be devalued, silenced, and overcome. We need to validate students' capacities for intellectual development at the beginning, not at the end, of their academic careers. This means that early on we must communicate that students of color are capable of academic thought and expression and that we believe and trust that their experience will guide them as they develop their intellectual capacities. An ideal classroom is one in which the teacher allows students to write about their culture and experiences, where the learning climate encourages creativity and freedom of expression, where teachers help students see the connection between what is taught and what is experienced in real life. We must find ways to change the linear model of teaching, where knowledge flows only from teacher to student. Instead, we must focus on collaborative learning and dialogue that promotes critical thinking, interpretation, and diversity of opinion.

We must set high standards, while helping students to reach them. Most faculty fail to give students the support they need in order to break free from belief systems that stifle their creativity. For example, many nontraditional students who come to college believe they cannot succeed, that their academic skills are not well developed, that they cannot compete with other students, that their perspectives are not valued in college, and/or that they will be "just a number" in college.

When I talk with college faculty, I often hear how they are tired of spoon-feeding students, how they have had to lower their standards, how students aren't motivated, how students don't care. Yet when I tell them that they must help and nurture these students, they balk. Most faculty believe that college students should be held accountable for their own actions, no matter what their past experience has been. While there is some truth to this, I agree with the authors of *Women's Ways of Knowing* (Belenky, Clinchy, Goldberger, and Tarule, 1986) that we need to find ways of caring that make the ones we care for stronger rather than weaker. Taking care need not necessarily equate to taking over. We need to create ways to look after our students so that they may develop the strength needed to assume responsibility for their own learning.

Most important, we must stop inflicting pain on students by demeaning and devaluing their past. If I had allowed myself to be molded into a student who rejects her past in order to attain success, I never would have been able to give something back that would strengthen my community. Recently, I decided to return to the Southwest, in large part to be closer to the people and the issues to which I am most committed. My academic success has made my parents proud of me, even when they don't fully understand what I do or what I write. And I am most proud of them for enduring an often agonizing experience with me.

Today we are witnessing the power of diversity. If higher education has up until now been able to validate scholarship "boys and girls" only when they have paid the high price of disconnection with their culture, it will become increasingly difficult to continue to do so. There are more and more of us (including white men and women) who are not buying into this flawed model of academic success. In the 1990s, as our numbers multiply, our power grows. If the academy refuses to change, we will change it. We will claim the curriculum, for we have always been a part of history, science, math, music, art, and literature. We will change teaching and learning to accommodate diversity. We will find our voice and use it to assert our rights and control our destiny.

I do not hunger for the past; it is always with me. Instead, I yearn for the future and believe that the time will come when higher education will be served by caring faculty, counselors, and administrators who know that they must do, not what is "politically correct," but what is morally and ethically the right thing. Many more like me will come to partake of the academy, classic scholarship men and women who leave home to find success in an alien land. We will change the academy, even as the academy changes us. And more and more of us will experience academic success—with few, if any, regrets.

References

Belenky, M. F., Clinchy, B. M., Goldberger, N. R., and Tarule, J. M. *Women's Ways of Knowing: The Development of Self, Voice, and Mind.* New York: Basic Books, 1986.

Galarza, E. "Institutional Deviancy: The Mexican American Experience." In *Mexican Ameri-*

can *Mental Health Issues: Present Realities and Future Strategies.* Boulder, Colo.: Western Interstate Commission for Higher Education, 1970.

Hoggart, R. *The Uses of Literacy: Aspects of Working-Class Life, With Special Reference to Publications and Entertainments.* New York: Oxford University Press, 1970.

Madrid, A. "Diversity and Its Discontents." *Academe,* 1990, 76 (6), 15–19.

Rodriguez, R. "Going Home Again: The New American Scholarship Boy." *American Scholar,* 1975, 44 (1), 15–28.

Rodriguez, R. *Hunger of Memory: The Education of Richard Rodriguez—An Autobiography.* Boston: Godine, 1982.

LAURA I. RENDÓN is associate research professor in the Division of Educational Leadership and Policy Studies at Arizona State University and has taught at North Carolina State University, the University of South Carolina, the University of Michigan, and Pennsylvania State University.

*One Latina student found ways to build a bridge between her
traditional world and that of a modern, cosmopolitan college.*

Reflections: Bridging Cultures

Julia Lara

Thirteen years have elapsed since I was a college student, first at a
community college and later in a private elite northeastern college. As I
look back at the central issues that shaped my experiences during those
years, two themes best typify this period of my life: transition and marginality. The transition from a familiar, reassuring, and traditional Latino
culture to the unknown and unpredictable world of modern North American college life placed me in a marginal situation relative to both cultures.
On the one hand, my experiences in college changed me in ways not fully
understood by my family; on the other, many people on campus were
unable to acknowledge and accept my cultural, linguistic, and racial
reality. In this chapter, I share thoughts about the states of transition and
marginality that I experienced during the college years.

Life at Community College

Going to college as an immigrant student did not at first create emotional
stress or tension between my family and myself. This was because I began
my college career at a community college. As a commuter student, going
to and from the community college campus was not very different from
going to and from high school. I came home every afternoon and participated in the same family activities that I had while in high school, and I
continued to conform to my family's expectations. From their point of
view, not much had changed.

 Although my parents knew little about community colleges and the
students they served, they were proud that I had been accepted. They (and
I) saw the community college as an opportunity. My father, with whom I

lived at the time, had not graduated from high school in the Dominican Republic. Instead, conditions compelled him to leave school early in order to help sustain his family. My mother had faced similar circumstances. Thus, even had I not gone beyond high school, they would have been satisfied that I had reached a level of academic training that they had not been able to achieve in their home country.

As a female of Hispanic background, I had been raised in a traditional and protective environment. As working-class immigrants, my parents did not know how to negotiate with such social institutions as the schools and city government. This gave me some freedom or decision-making latitude early in my school career. My father rarely examined what went on (socially or instructionally) at the schools I attended. I used to sign my own report cards, and whenever possible I complied with any written requests sent by the school to my parents. This pattern lasted throughout my school career. In hindsight, the disadvantage was that I received little guidance from my father or anyone else in the family concerning school-related matters. The opposite was true when it came to interactions with the world outside of school. During the high school years I was not allowed to date, go to parties, go out on weekend trips with my friends, or sleep at my girlfriends' homes overnight. I recall that while in high school I attempted to stay at my best friend's house, but my older brother, with whom I lived at that time, would not allow it and came to my girlfriend's house to pick me up. I was terribly embarrassed by the whole affair and went home in tears.

While attending a community college did not significantly change my home life, it did change how I viewed myself and the world around me. I was fortunate to be one of a group of students who were "adopted" by three innovative educators committed to the notion of empowering working-class immigrant and minority students. We came to believe that our experiences, thoughts, and beliefs were legitimate and to reject the negative stereotypes often attributed to members of our gender, social class, or ethnic group. Of equal importance, we realized that despite our own racial and cultural differences, we had common experiences that could serve as the basis for providing some service to our communities. The process of empowerment involved reading and discussing the works of such great social thinkers as Camus, Fanon, Marx, and others; making decisions about the focus of student programs and activities; enrolling in a political science course at Yale University while still at community college and there discovering that the children of the elite were not inherently smarter than we were; and engaging in discussions with some of the more provocative and controversial figures of the time. These and other experiences were instrumental in our personal and intellectual growth.

The issue of separation from family and a familiar environment was raised during my second year in the community college. I was presented with an opportunity to transfer to a four-year liberal arts college in another state. The experiences in the community college had enhanced my self-esteem and led me to believe that I could reach academic and professional goals higher than I had previously thought possible. Indeed, when I had told my high school counselor that I wanted to study medicine, she replied that I was only slightly above average in IQ and that she doubted seriously that I could make it. I was disheartened by her assessment, but her position gave her credibility, and I had abandoned the idea of becoming a doctor. However, the opportunity to attend a four-year liberal arts college with a premedical program rekindled my desire to pursue medicine as a career.

The possibility of achieving my career goals was not the only motivating factor. I wanted to leave home. I wanted to be in a situation where I would be free to make decisions, to have control of my immediate environment, and to be alone. But I could not share these feelings with members of my family. I knew that they would wonder what had happened to me. "Has she become ungrateful of our efforts?" they would ask. "Is she being influenced negatively by American cultural norms and beliefs?" I felt guilty and ashamed for wanting to leave because I understood that my family had provided all that they could, given their circumstances. Yet I knew that leaving home to go to college was an opportunity to explore a world that at that time was alien to me. I was uncertain about what I would find, yet I wanted to experience it.

Fitting In

As a Latina of African descent, I encountered a number of challenges in a private, predominantly white institution. These challenges centered around how one survived intellectually and emotionally in an environment that devalued one's contribution because of one's race and cultural background; how African American students ignored or rejected the cultural and linguistic uniqueness of the Latino students; and how other Latinos who were not of African descent rejected Afro-Latino students.

I arrived at this small upper-class college feeling good about being there and with high expectations about what I would be able to accomplish. As a transfer student, I did not have the option of easing into the more advanced and intellectually demanding courses. I had to learn quickly to compete with classmates who came from more advantaged backgrounds. As a premed student, I took required courses such as calculus and chemistry, and I worked hard to do well in them. However, by the end of the first semester I realized that despite my self-confidence, I lacked the quantitative preparation to pursue a career in medicine. This was a great disappointment. I felt I had "let down" my advisers at the community college who had been instrumental in expanding my worldview and in building my confidence. Ironically, my high school counselor had been right: I did not have the mathematical background to be a premed. But I also knew that she was wrong about the source of the problem: it wasn't a question of IQ; it was the poor academic training I had received during my precollegiate years.

Switching majors, I selected a field that was of interest although not my first preference. I decided to pursue a career teaching political science at the university level. Again, there were moments of self-doubt. Could I meet this goal? Did I have the "smarts" to do it? After all, in all of my classes I was surrounded by upper-middle-class students who were comfortable culturally and intellectually in that environment. They were quite different from the working-class students I had met at the community college, who had been products of an urban public school system. For example, in social gatherings my new classmates engaged frequently in small talk that to many of us from less privileged backgrounds seemed trite and irrelevant. In class, these students were skillful at embellishing the discussion of any given issue. Yet they did not draw conclusions that were any more profound than those of us who got to the point quickly.

I learned through my interaction with white students to be distrustful of them. While socially they were friendly and seemed interested in me as an individual and in my experience as a minority student, in the competitive context of the college classroom these students underrated the intellectual ability of students from minority backgrounds. This often led to disrespectful and dishonest behavior by the Anglo students. I recall being in a senior seminar in political philosophy where students were required to critique each other's work, both orally and in writing. Students in this class often got together to discuss their understanding of the political philosophers whose writings we were asked to analyze and interpret. I shared with one male white student the paper that I was scheduled to present and defend in the seminar and asked for his opinion. His response was that the paper was fine, that he, too, had some difficulties with the ideas put forth by the philosopher, and that he did not find any major weaknesses in the paper. I walked into the seminar with some apprehension but thinking that others (particularly the student with whom I had talked) had also had difficulties with the work of the philosopher and that I was therefore not alone. Once in the classroom, this student proceeded to expose weaknesses in my analysis that he had not mentioned during our previous discussions. I was shocked, hurt, and embarrassed by the betrayal. It became obvious to me that my feelings did not matter to him. His objective was to enhance his stature within the class.

I also learned that it was difficult to maintain one's ethnic identity in an environment that viewed the world in terms of black and white. I was generally accepted by the African American students because I was black. But with a few exceptions, these students had little interest in the Spanish language or in Latino culture. While cognizant of my cultural linkages with the African American students and feeling a part of this population, I also wanted these students to understand that for Latinos the language and cultural legacy of their land, in my case the Dominican Republic, were a source of pride, as was the recognition that there were strong cultural linkages between Latinos from the Caribbean islands and African Americans. I recall working hard to organize the African American Cultural Day celebration at the college, but getting little support from the African American students when a similar event was organized to celebrate Latino culture. These experiences taught me that despite some measure of cultural affinity, African American students were, after all, Americans and often did not understand the immigrant student, whether or not that student was of African descent.

On the other hand, the Latino students had little interaction with the Afro-Latino students. In spite of the fact that we shared a language and in some instances similar cultural norms and values, they viewed me as not really Latina. After all, I was black, was comfortable with the African American students, and shared their perspectives, particularly those concerning relations between black and white students on campus. Thus, I experienced a bicultural, bilingual state of being with which I ultimately came to terms by the end of my school career. Coming to terms with this duality meant that I had to become more knowledgeable of my historical and cultural antecedents and then, armed with that knowledge, maintain a strong belief in the importance of accepting and affirming the cultural and linguistic uniqueness that we all possess in this multiracial and multicultural society.

Issues of Identity

These examples of lack of understanding across cultures but within race stand out because they are central to the experience of immigrant students who want to retain some of the cultural and linguistic legacy of their native land. These are, in essence, issues of identity.

As a mother, wife, professional woman, and community volunteer, I now look back at these experiences as valuable lessons that have influenced my life and work since college. My current work in educational administration is motivated by the same desires that motivated my mentors in the community college: empowerment of those who are disenfranchised in this society. Moreover, bridging two cultures that are often at odds in the urban context remains a challenge. In conversations with immigrant youth who are "marginal" in the same way I was, I often talk about how I reconciled the racial and cultural dilemma of the high school and college years. I hope that sharing these experiences will reassure these youths by showing them that others have met these challenges successfully.

JULIA LARA is senior project associate at the Council of Chief State School Officers in Washington, D.C., and is completing a doctorate in bilingual and multicultural education at George Mason University, Virginia. She is also a graduate of Staten Island Community College, Middlebury College, and Columbia University.

Miami-Dade Community College uses a comprehensive system of academic support to counteract the problems that first-generation students frequently encounter.

The Challenge of First-Generation College Students: A Miami-Dade Perspective

Eduardo J. Padron

The majority of American colleges and universities have no precise data available to determine how many of their students are first-generation students. Miami-Dade Community College (MDCC) is no exception. However, the demographic characteristics of the community and of the students can serve as indicators of the proportion of students who are the first in their family to attend college.

The Wolfson campus of Miami-Dade Community College, located in downtown Miami, is the only urban college campus in the greater Miami area. The average enrollment for the Fall and Winter term is slightly over 10,000. Students at the campus represent forty-two different languages and 120 countries; foreign and refugee students constitute 18 percent of the enrollment. More than 60 percent of Wolfson campus students receive need-based state and federal financial aid. Two-thirds of entering freshmen test deficient in one or more basic skills at the time of enrollment. Sixty-five percent of the students have a native language other than English. The ethnic composition of the campus is 11.4 percent black, 73.5 percent Hispanic, 14.1 percent white, and 1 percent other. Sixty-one percent of students are female, and 39 percent male. Students aged fourteen to twenty

I would like to thank Dr. Castell Bryant, Dr. Raul De La Cruz, Nora Hendrix, Dr. Mercedes Sandoval, and Dr. Jose Vicente for sharing their experiences and insights with me. I would also like to thank Sherry Braswell for assistance in preparing and editing this chapter.

comprise 26.3 percent of the student population; 28.5 percent are twenty-one to twenty-five; 16.8 percent are twenty-six to thirty; 10.7 percent are thirty-one to thirty-five; 6.8 percent are thirty-six to forty; and 10.9 percent are over forty-one. Only 29 percent of students hold no jobs, while 16 percent work one to twenty hours per week, 14 percent work twenty-one to thirty hours per week, 24 percent work thirty-one to forty hours per week, and 18 percent work more than forty hours per week.

A 1990 survey by the U.S. Census Bureau of twenty-five-year-olds in the area revealed that 89 percent of whites, 60 percent of Hispanics, and 56 percent of blacks had a high school education or more. However, only 28 percent of whites, 11 percent of Hispanics, and 11.3 percent of blacks had completed college. Many students test deficient in basic skills after they have taken the appropriate courses in high school and failed to learn these skills, but a large number of them test deficient because they have not taken college preparatory classes, such as algebra and geometry, prior to enrolling in college.

While a college student population cannot be considered equivalent to a random sample of the city's population, neither does it seem reasonable to assume that the majority of these students, especially given their lack of academic preparation for college, come from the small percentage of college-educated Miami families. Families in the greater Miami area may send their children to private universities, a public university, or one of several campuses of the community college, all of which are within the county, in addition to institutions of higher learning elsewhere. Since college-educated parents might reasonably be expected to send their offspring to a four-year institution immediately after high school graduation, the first-generation student population would be more concentrated at community colleges. We thus estimate that a substantial majority of students here are first-generation students. Formal reports from faculty and administrators support this estimate.

Characteristics of First-Generation MDCC Students

The most commonly reported characteristic of these students has been a need for more guidance, both academic and personal, than other students require. A psychology professor commented that they often came to him with their fears and insecurities. The campus dean of students, Castell Bryant, has observed that a large percentage of these students are often intimidated and bewildered by the educational system and do not understand when the system can be flexible and when it cannot. As an example, Bryant cited a request by a single mother to retake an exam. The night preceding the student's exam, a portion of the roof of her apartment had collapsed, sending down debris inches away from her sleeping infant. She had spent the night in a roofless apartment with a frightened, crying child.

In the morning she went to her class, took the exam, and not surprisingly, did poorly on it. The student did not know how to take appropriate action—that is, to call the instructor, explain the circumstances, and postpone the test. She simply assumed that because the test was scheduled for that morning, she had to take it at that time.

A major problem of first-generation students at MDCC is that their home atmosphere is often the antithesis of a good learning and studying environment. They have no designated place or time to study at home; they may read their textbooks while sitting on a couch in a room with inadequate lighting, for example. They often do not know how to reconcile the demands of their home life with the demands of their studies. Students report having conflicting demands—being told, for example, that they must baby-sit younger siblings at times when they should be in class. They often come from cultures that regard higher education as frivolous. Students who are single mothers have stated that their parents criticize them for attending college; the parents feel that the single mother should spend all her time caring for her baby.

Parents and siblings can frequently be nonsupportive and even obstructionist. For example, among first-generation college students who have an older sibling who did not attend college, the latter often subjects the student to ridicule and insult by claiming, "Now you're in college, you think you're better than me." Other pressures can be more subtle but equally disturbing. One student asked for advice when, after working for the summer to save tuition money, his mother began to badger him to use the money to buy a car so that she would no longer have to take cabs when doing her shopping.

Since many MDCC students are immigrants, there is a high percentage of older students at the campus. They frequently enroll to learn English and later go on to take other classes. Many of them have children in the public school system, and those children are the only familial support system they have. MDCC also has occurrences of two or more generations of the same family attending college simultaneously. A mother and daughter may attend simultaneously, for example; at every graduation there are usually a few instances of a parent and child each receiving a degree. In these cases, each student can reinforce the other's determination to persist in college, but neither has previous experience with higher education and therefore lacks familiarity with the college system.

This lack of adequate familial support for education typifies some alarming changes that have occurred in the last two decades. In the Miami community, there is the perception that the Hispanic immigrants, especially Cubans, of the 1960s were much better educated than immigrants of the last decade; in fact, the higher-than-average educational attainment of Cuban immigrants prior to 1980 has been well documented (Jaffe, Cullen, and Boswell, 1980). There has been a general change of attitude on the part of recent immigrants as well. A professor at the Little Havana outreach center noted grimly that immigrant parents in the late 1960s, when they were unable to subsidize their offsprings' college education entirely on their own, would literally scrub floors so that their children in college would only have to work a minimum number of hours to pay tuition costs. Now, she says, parents sometimes allow their children in college to hold full-time jobs so that the parents can purchase a new car.

Even more worrisome to Bryant at the Wolfson campus are the increasing numbers of first-generation students whose parents are indifferent or even antagonistic toward the educational system. Almost always, she states, the school system failed these parents when they were students, and they dropped out in the tenth or eleventh grade with their actual skills at a fifth- or sixth-grade level. These parents are most difficult to reach and can diminish their children's educational aspirations and opportunities (Mare, 1980). By not monitoring or comprehending their children's progress through the secondary school system, they fail to insist that their children take college preparatory classes. Subsequently, even when the child decides to attend college in the face of parental discouragement, that child finds himself or herself inadequately prepared and can feel humiliated by not performing well on placement tests. Such students must often spend an entire academic year taking college preparatory classes before they are actually ready to "enter" college, even though they may have been on the college campus for that year. The resulting feelings of inadequacy make retaining these students even more problematic.

The attitudes of the students themselves toward higher education can also be disconcerting to faculty. Raul De La Cruz, a faculty member in arts and sciences at MDCC, believes that first-generation students are more likely to possess a "union-card mentality" about education. The degree that they seek is not valued for the sake of knowledge or education but rather simply as a document the students must have in order to make a better living than their parents. While many students can certainly have this kind of pragmatic attitude toward education (Fligstein and Fernandez, 1985), De La Cruz more often finds it necessary to explain to first-generation students in particular that although a degree may suffice to obtain an entry-level position in business, retaining the position will depend on the knowledge and energy that they bring to the job.

Both faculty and administration believe that first-generation students are more likely to externalize responsibility and blame when they do not do well in a course. For example, they are more apt to blame external circumstances than to consider their own commitment to the course or their study habits. As another example, many first-generation students receive financial aid but have distorted perceptions about their responsibilities and those of the faculty regarding the financial aid. Faculty cite the common occurrence of students calling them after the end of the term to complain about their grade for the course. Often the students justify their complaint by saying, "I needed an A in this course because of my scholarship." De La Cruz deals with this type of complaint by reminding students that scholarships are given because of good grades, not the other way around, and that faculty have no obligation to give them high grades.

Equally important, De La Cruz feels, is that while first-generation students may have unique problems, they also have characteristics that create positive interactions with faculty. They seem more receptive to alternative methods of teaching and teaming than students from college-educated families. Because attending college is not something that they have taken for granted throughout their lives, they frequently appear more motivated than other students. It is easier to be a role model for them. De La Cruz reports that many of his Hispanic students, for whom he may be the first Hispanic educator they have known, come to him and say, "I want to be you." He explains to them that they must develop their own adult identities, which can include being Hispanic professionals, but that they cannot and should not become an exact duplicate of him. He and other faculty members acknowledge that serving as role models for these students motivates them as instructors. However, they caution that it is also important for the classroom to have students who come from educated backgrounds. As De La Cruz notes, these students "give me a more critical appraisal than the first-generation students do." It may well be that the mix of first-generation students and students from educated families creates a more dynamic learning atmosphere than would otherwise exist.

Assisting First-Generation Students

The Wolfson campus has evolved over the years into a place that attracts a large number of minority students. The strategies that have been implemented to recruit and retain these students also work for first-generation students. Because minority students (and correspondingly, first-generation students) tend to be less aware of educational opportunities, a great deal of energy has been put into disseminating information about the college. The basic information groundwork is supplemented by working with feeder high schools to recruit students following high school graduation and with the business community to attract older students who are already members of the work force. After students enroll, the college makes a concerted effort to keep them enrolled. Particularly within the last ten years, Wolfson has focused on creating an inviting atmosphere for students from a wide variety of backgrounds. Part of this effort has involved establishing a less formal ambiance than one might expect at a college. More structured methods of retaining students include targeted programs for students at high risk of dropping out. With the various recruitment and retention programs that we have in place, we feel that we can serve first-generation students well.

Recruiting First-Generation Students. MDCC Wolfson focuses on aggressively recruiting students who otherwise might not attend college. Many of these programs are aimed specifically at black and Hispanic students, who are more likely to come from families with no direct experience with higher education, while other programs work with personnel in secondary schools. One such program is the Black Student Recruitment Program, which consists of a six-week training and work-experience program for counselors and administrators who work with black students at each of Wolfson's feeder high schools. The program familiarizes high school personnel with the college and with trends in the education of black students. The counselors work on campus for six weeks and then recruit students from their schools when they return. The program encourages relationships between college staff and high school faculty in order to promote the enrollment of black students both immediately and in the future.

The Jump Start program targets students who have test scores and grade point averages sufficient for college work but who are ambivalent about their plans after they graduate from high school. These students are referred to Wolfson by their schools and classified as "high-risk" students. The program offers six academic credits of summer instruction, including three credits in a college survival skills course. This course provides support services and close personal tutorial and advisory services to the students.

Similarly, the Summer Institute is a free support services program developed to equip students with the necessary tools to meet the challenges of college life. This course enhances student study skills and provides some basic computer instruction. Highly motivated recently graduated high school students, who have already applied for admission to colleges, are invited to participate in the Summer Institute to ease their transition into college once they matriculate in the Fall term. Recently graduated high school students who have not yet applied to college for admission and are undecided in terms of whether they'll seek employment or attend college are referred to the Jump Start program by school counselors. The program components consist of academics and enrichment activities all geared toward motivating these students to pursue a college education and exposing them to the college experience.

Although these programs and others like them are useful in reaching some high school students, their personalized nature prevents them from being sufficient for large-scale recruiting. Therefore, we believe in letting the community at large know about our educational opportunities. Student services personnel visit feeder high schools on a regular basis to acquaint them with the college and its programs. Senior administrators and the public relations staff have established ties with local media and work with them to publicize the college. Also, faculty and staff who are involved in community groups and causes often receive calls from fellow group or committee members, requesting information or assistance for a relative.

The outreach center in Little Havana, called the InterAmerican Center, plays a vital role in attracting first-generation students, many of them fairly recent immigrants. The center's bilingual programs, staff, and atmosphere make communication possible for students and family members with limited English. Jose Vicente, dean of the InterAmerican Center, notes that he uses every available opportunity for media exposure. Radio and television shows, especially those conducted in Spanish, present many opportunities to promote educational achievement for Hispanics. Vicente uses information about salary levels and the skills needed for jobs to emphasize to non-English speakers that education is a necessity for their children and can be beneficial to the parents as well. Fliers are printed both in English and Spanish and distributed throughout the neighborhood. The center also tracks applicants for admission, sending letters to those who were admitted but who failed to register for classes within two terms.

The goal of Wolfson's marketing strategies is not just to promote enrollment at the college but also to educate the population about the realities of work-force demands. The community must be made aware of the demand for more educated workers, the existence of college programs, and the availability of financial aid for those who qualify.

Retaining First-Generation Students. Retention efforts actually begin prior to official enrollment. Because the college feels that a less intimidating setting is an essential part of retaining high-risk students such as those who are first-generation attendees, the traditional college admissions office does not exist here. Students who wish to enroll at the college for the first time go to the New Student Center. By design, the center contains no counters, nothing that can create a physical barrier between the staff and the prospective students. An applicant who walks in is greeted by a receptionist, who gives him or her an admissions form. The applicant sits at a table with a staff member and completes the form. The staff members are bilingual so that students can ask questions in their native language, thus making them feel more at ease and more apt to identify with the college. At peak registration times, several applicants may be at the same table with each staff member, but even under these circumstances the setting is much more individualized than in most admissions offices. The aim is to prevent the admissions procedure from being an impersonal process during which a student fills out a form alone and drops it off with an anonymous clerk.

After students are enrolled, the campus seeks to retain them by monitoring their academic progress and keeping students apprised of problems. All classes participate in the Academic Alert system, which identifies at midterm those students with weak academic progress and with sporadic attendance records. For each student in each class, faculty members provide a progress assessment and an evaluation of attendance. This information, along with computer-stored student characteristics, is used to generate individualized letters for students who are not making sufficient progress. Counselors also call students at home and urge them to improve their academic standing; they schedule appointments with students to discuss the reasons for any problem. The Academic Alert system helps reassure first-generation students that the college is concerned about them as individuals. It also circumvents their reluctance to seek tutorial assistance on their own initiative.

As part of its commitment to retain high-risk students, Wolfson utilizes proactive mentor programs that team faculty or staff with individual students to provide extra counseling and academic support. Students who are identified during the admissions process as high risk are required to take a college orientation course, which teaches them some of the practical skills needed to succeed at college. This course is particularly useful for first-generation students, who lack basic familiarity with standard college practices, as it teaches them everything from how to drop or add a course to how to identify those administrative and support personnel they might need to consult under different circumstances. Programs that assist high-risk students as they progress through college include the Black Student Retention Program, the Hispanic Student Success Program, and COPE (Comprehensive Opportunity to Pursue Excellence). Each of these programs enables the student to find advice and supportive communication in times and areas of need. The COPE program has several components designed to address different areas of student need. For example, students receive two free hours of tutoring per week in basic English and math skills. In addition, because students are often passive about seeking academic advisement, faculty members who are assigned as mentors contact their designated students at least twice a month and invite them to come in for discussion. In a study that Wolfson conducted in 1988 (Alvarez, 1988), students who participated in these programs showed a significantly lower rate of withdrawal from college than students in a control group.

Another component still in its testing stage is the use of clustering for at least one academic year. Students who are clustered are assigned to as many classes together as possible in the hope that they will evolve into a team that can give each other academic and perhaps social support. A proposed program would bring in family members for discussion with counselors in order to emphasize to the families the importance of allowing first-generation students sufficient time at home to study.

Wolfson also increases retention by creating an atmosphere that demonstrates appreciation for different cultures. Celebrations such as Hispanic Heritage Month, Black Heritage Month, and International Month are held each year. The rationale for these celebrations is fairly simple: rather than trying to ignore the ethnic and cultural differences of the students, the campus celebrates them, at the same time giving students the opportunity to learn about the customs and cultures of their fellow students. First-generation students experience relief that the campus regards their cultural background as important.

It is of great importance that the college staff reflect at all levels the community they serve. Since so many first-generation students are minority students, the problems that they face will only be compounded if they find themselves in an academic environment that lacks adequate numbers of positive role models for them. Ethnic diversity among faculty, staff, and administration will reinforce to these students that perseverance in higher education brings professional status and recognition. Particularly in urban settings such as Miami with ethnically and culturally diverse populations, establishing and maintaining a similar diversity among college staff is an imperative. The Wolfson campus has distinguished itself for having made great strides in this area. As of 1991, blacks constituted 17.9 percent of the administration, 26.5 percent of the classified staff, and 11.2 percent of faculty. Hispanics accounted for 48.2 percent of the administration, 60.3 percent of the classified staff, and 38.5 percent of the faculty.

Conclusion

First-generation students can best be served by strategies that counteract the problems and weaknesses that many bring with them to higher education. Recruitment efforts to target them must also involve targeting appropriate family members who can provide support. Retention efforts should focus on involving the student in the classroom and on the campus as much as possible. Special support services to provide additional counseling and tutoring can greatly enhance the progress of first-generation students. While the student population at MDCC may be atypical of many community colleges because of its overwhelmingly large minority and immigrant enrollment, the programs outlined here can be duplicated or adapted on other campuses. However, the administration of the college must be willing to set the standard through its actions and policies. Ultimately, these strategies, as well as those successfully employed at other colleges, must be given serious consideration by any college that seeks to provide first-generation students with the academic and social support they need in order to succeed.

References

Alvarez, R. "Proactive Facilitation with Refugee/Immigrant Students: An Attrition Prevention Study." Unpublished doctoral dissertation, University of Miami, 1988.

Fligstein, N., and Fernandez, R. M. "Hispanics and Education." In P.S.J. Cafferty and W. C. McCready (eds.), *Hispanics in the United States: A New Social Agenda*. New Brunswick, N.J.: Transaction Books, 1985.

Jaffe, A. J., Cullen, R. M., and Boswell, T. D. *The Changing Demography of Spanish Americans*. New York: Academic Press, 1980.

Mare, R. "Social Background and School Continuation Decisions." *Journal of the American Statistical Association*, 1980, 75, 295–305.

EDUARDO J. PADRON is president and chief executive officer of the Wolfson campus of Miami-Dade Community College, and he serves as chairman-elect of the Hispanic Association of Colleges and Universities.

•

At LaGuardia Community College, the needs of first-generation students are met with creative initiatives—alternative high schools, programs in critical thinking and neighborhood history, and a partnership with Vassar College to enhance transfer opportunities.

Transforming Educational Dreams into Educational Reality

John Chaffee

"What is a woman who is black and Hispanic and from the slums of Brooklyn doing attending a school like Yale?" asks Dolores Colon-Montalvo, and the answer is obvious. A first-generation college student, Dolores entered college at age forty after raising two children; she exudes dynamism, determination, and unabashed wonder at what she has accomplished. For every Dolores Colon-Montalvo, however, scores of other first-generation students have seen their dreams end in what for them is an alien culture. For higher education, the critical question is how the development of first-generation college students can be fostered. At LaGuardia Community College, a branch of the City University of New York (CUNY), we have been asking and answering this question for the past twenty years.

LaGuardia was founded in 1971, the same year that CUNY adopted an open-admissions policy that guaranteed enrollment to all students possessing a high school diploma or graduate equivalency degree. From the outset, LaGuardia knew that first-generation college students would be its primary constituency. This is still the case, with the most recent analysis of the LaGuardia population yielding the following profile. It is an ethnically diverse campus: Caucasian students comprise 18 percent of the population; blacks, 29 percent; Hispanics, 33 percent; and Asians, 13 percent. Fifty percent of entering students are foreign born, and the population is largely "nontraditional": 48 percent of entering students are over twenty-one years old, 69 percent did not come directly from high school, and 64 percent are female. Finally, 85 percent test in need of remediation in writing, reading, oral skills, mathematics, or some combination of these areas.

In order to meet the educational challenges presented by this population, LaGuardia has developed a broad range of pioneering programs, including the Middle College and International High School, the Critical-Thinking Program, the Speech Communication Program, the Neighborhood History Program, and the Vassar College–LaGuardia "Exploring Transfer" Program.

The LaGuardia Middle College and International High School

"You must expect the unexpected, for you cannot find it by search or trail" (Heraclitus, cited in Kirk and Raven, 1966, p. 127).

Many potential first-generation college students never expect to attend college nor find the trail that leads to postsecondary education. To assist students whose backgrounds are not consistent with high educational aspirations, LaGuardia developed linkages with a group of local high schools and created two innovative high schools on the LaGuardia campus itself. Initiated by Janet Lieberman in 1974, the LaGuardia Middle College targets high-risk students drawn from throughout New York City. Once admitted, students enter an educational environment far different from the one that helped to put them at risk. Small classes and attentive teachers draw them in as members of a learning community.

Collaborative learning activities combined with a flexible, open structure help students develop into mature, responsible individuals. Because the school is integrated into the college campus, students become familiar with the college culture and the possibilities it offers. Qualified students are permitted to enroll in college courses, and every graduate is guaranteed admission to LaGuardia Community College. Instead of becoming entangled in the educationally regressive influences of their high schools and neighborhoods, students are given the opportunity to emulate a different set of values and role models. As Middle College principal Cecelia Cullen explains, "students tend to copy the behavior of the community college student and rise to that level" (Cullen, 1989, p. 3).

The International High School, created in 1985, applies the successful Middle College model to another at-risk population: recent immigrants with limited English proficiency. Also situated on the LaGuardia campus, this school uses the strategies of the Middle College but combines the study of all subject matter with intensive instruction in English. Faculty across the curriculum integrate English-as-a-second-language (ESL) techniques into their courses, thereby accelerating the development of students' language abilities.

The impact of these two alternative high schools on the lives of at-risk and first-generation potential college students has been impressive: attrition is almost nonexistent among the 900 students, and over 90 percent of the graduates continue their education at college campuses.

The LaGuardia Critical-Thinking Program

"Without the breath of life, the human body is a corpse; without thinking, the human mind is dead" (Arendt, 1978, p. 4).

An academic culture that prizes the life of the mind and the development of the individual into a reflective, mature thinker is foreign to many first-generation students. Moreover, many college educators believe that courses that stimulate the development of students' critical-thinking abilities should be reserved for more advanced students who have already learned "the basics"—that is, literacy and the general core of knowledge supposedly imparted through introductory-level courses. We have found this assumption to be pedagogically unsound, for it short-circuits the educational careers of many first-generation students who become disaffected before they can be introduced to the spirit of inquiry and who have not yet developed a more mature sense of self and intellectual commitment.

In contrast, faculty at LaGuardia view learning to think critically as an essential and powerful vehicle for developing cognitive and literacy abilities at every level of education. In 1979, I developed the Critical-Thinking Skills course, which was designed to introduce entering students to the cognitive process and help them develop the higher-order thinking and literacy abilities needed for academic and career success. Funded by two grants from the National Endowment for the Humanities, the initial seed has developed into an interdisciplinary program that involves over 800 students annually and is taught by faculty from a wide variety of disciplines.

The LaGuardia model is based on the assumption that becoming a critical thinker does not simply involve developing discrete intellectual abilities; rather, it involves developing insight, reflective judgment, informed beliefs, and a willingness to explore diverse perspectives carefully. As students develop their critical-thinking abilities, they also grow as individuals, developing the qualities of maturity, open-mindedness, responsibility, initiative, and a sense that they can control the direction of their lives through the choices that they make. In the words of one LaGuardia student, "the words *critical thinking* will never leave my vocabulary because by learning how to organize my ideas, support my point of view with reasons, and try to solve my problems rationally, I have learned more effective ways of dealing with my life, my children, and my schoolwork" (Chaffee, 1985, p. 21).

At LaGuardia, critical thinking is fostered through the use of teaching "pairs": sections of Critical-Thinking Skills are joined with other courses selected from a variety of academic areas such as English, reading, oral communication, mathematics, and social science. Students enrolled in a course pairing take both courses, and faculty pairs meet weekly to redesign their courses, if necessary, and refine their teaching methodology with the aim of fostering critical-thinking abilities.

The Critical-Thinking Program has been evaluated positively by both the Educational Testing Service and the National Endowment for the Humanities. The program appears to have succeeded in meeting its three primary objectives: to develop literacy, reasoning and problem-solving abilities, and critical attitudes. For example, students enrolled in the program have demonstrated accelerated language development, nearly doubling the collegewide pass rate on standardized writing and reading examinations. In addition, according to Garlie Forehand, director of research at the Educational Testing Service and the primary evaluator of the program, "at the general level, teachers perceive more respect for the thinking process, more tendency to bring a habit of thinking to their classes. At the specific level, teachers reported instances of transfer of such skills as breaking problems into parts, classifying, organization of thought, asking questions, separating facts from opinions, and assessing alternative points of view" (Chaffee, 1985, p. 58).

Since fundamental thinking abilities and critical abilities work together and interact in complex ways, students do not learn them in a skill-by-skill fashion. Instead, as developmental theory predicts and faculty analyses confirm, students in the program seem to be undergoing a developmental process in which skills, attitudes, and perceptions are progressively reorganized into new cognitive patterns. This leads to breakthrough or "aha" experiences as students discover new methods and abilities, revealed in student comments like "It expands thinking—like a tool"; "part of my brain awakened"; "it put a seed, a spark, in me" (Chaffee, 1985, p. 21).

The Speech and Communication Program

"The relations of word to thought and the creation of new concepts is a complex, delicate, and enigmatic process unfolding in our soul" (Tolstoy, cited in Vygotsky, 1978, p. 218).

The Speech Communication Program promotes intellectual development through an in-depth understanding of language. The program helps students to use words appropriately and coherently, an essential ingredient for professional success. Many first-generation students, both native and foreign born, display a variety of language and communication problems that limit their career opportunities and often result in destructive stereotyping. These difficulties include accented speech, nonstandard syntax, imprecise pronunciation, inadequate volume, poor resonance, and limited vocal expression.

Paradoxically, while most colleges provide substantive programs to develop students' abilities in writing and reading, they typically offer little to improve students' all-important speaking and communication abilities. Directed by Sandra Dickinson, the Speech Communication Program offers approximately fifty course sections each quarter, servicing various populations and addressing an array of students' speaking and communication problems. Basic Communication Strategies, for example, is a two-course sequence for Basic Skills students designed to promote standard language use; Oral Communication is designed to expand basic speaking skills in interpersonal, business, and public contexts. Communication and the Nonnative Speaker focuses on the specific needs of ESL students, while Voice and Diction provides a phonetic approach to modifying pronunciation patterns. Traditional speech courses in public speaking, business communication, debate and inquiry, and multicultural communication are also available.

The Speech Communication courses are supported by the Speech Center, an audiolingual and tutoring facility. The center accommodates laboratory classes, required by five of the program's courses, as well as individual students referred by faculty and staff. A speech referral system, staffed by faculty volunteers, evaluates students referred from other departments, tracks and documents use of the Speech Center, and records the progress made by students on their individual speech plans. Video technology is used in speech assessment, tutor training, and laboratory documentation, and specially created audiolingual tapes are used to improve students' pronunciation.

The intent of the Speech Communication Program is ambitious: "to understand patterns in language and speech, and to know how to use them appropriately in varied contexts, is a tool that lends power to students' communication and thinking" (Dickinson, 1991, p. 284).

The Neighborhood History Program

"If you can memorize it, it isn't history!" (Singer, 1988).

As outsiders to the culture of higher education, first-generation students often challenge the passive "information-transfer" model of education, in which material presented in lectures is re-presented on examinations. Rather, these students are likely to ask, "Why is it important to master this information?" In response to this question, Richard Lieberman, professor of history at LaGuardia and director of the F. H. LaGuardia and Wagner Archives, reconceptualized his teaching of history. Abandoning more traditional approaches, he used his courses to develop materials with his students that linked them more directly to their families and personal histories. As they explored the histories of their families and neighborhoods, students began to understand what it means to "think historically" and how history and its methodologies can help explain the events in their lives, as well as the larger social forces that have shaped and influenced those events.

These initial experiences led to six years of funding from the National Endowment for the Humanities for the purpose of engaging students in the study of history. Directed by Richard Lieberman and Janet Lieberman (no relation), the project used public exhibits, slide shows, oral history projects, and publications in order to show people (most with little or no exposure to higher education) how their lives and neighborhoods are a part of American history. Additional educational materials and a text, *City Limits* (Lieberman and Lieberman, 1983), were developed and incorporated into the curriculum. Furthermore, the LaGuardia and Wagner Archives, housed on the LaGuardia campus, afford students the opportunity to engage in historical research.

Participating in the historical process has had an illuminating and empowering effect on first-generation students. As Richard Lieberman explains, "our students experience change on a daily basis. The goal of history is to enable people to see that change is not capricious, that there are explanations which lend coherence and meaning to the events which shape our lives" (Lieberman, 1979, p. 7).

The Vassar College–LaGuardia Community College "Exploring Transfer" Program

"I have learned that there are two kinds of education in this country. The first is designed to train workers. The second is designed to educate thinkers and doers" (Nissman, 1987, p. 1).

The challenge for first-generation college students does not end once they successfully adapt to college, particularly if their institution is a public university or community college. Often the most capable of these students have fixed vocational goals. These goals seem lofty when measured by the expectations of their families but limited when measured in terms of the students' actual potential. When Dolores Colon-Montalvo and Sue Nissman entered their community college, an associate degree and perhaps a bachelor's from a public university marked the boundaries of their dreams. After completing the Vassar College–LaGuardia Community College "Exploring Transfer" Program, these boundaries were extended: Dolores transferred to Yale University, while Sue transferred to the Massachusetts Institute of Technology (MIT).

The "Exploring Transfer" Program, begun in 1985, is a collaboration between Vassar College and LaGuardia Community College designed to promote transfer possibilities for first-generation community college students. Participating students, selected for their academic promise, attend an intensive five-week program on the Vassar College campus. Funded by the Ford Foundation, the program introduces students to the experience of a four-year residential college, challenges their abilities through two rigorous, team-taught courses, makes them aware of the full range of transfer opportunities available to them, and helps them develop confidence in their abilities to achieve their goals. The program opens a new world to them and helps give them the tools to enter into and succeed in that new world.

The results of this collaborative initiative have been impressive. During the past six years, 264 students have successfully completed the program, and virtually all have transferred to four-year colleges, many to prestigious institutions such as Vassar, Yale, Middlebury College, Cornell University, and MIT. The effectiveness of the program derives from immersing students in the culture of a residential four-year college. As they absorb the philosophy and possibilities of this culture, students can begin to apply the implications to their own lives. In the words of Janet Lieberman, a founder of the program and recipient of the Charles A. Dana award for its development, "direct experience is a powerful learning technique. It is particularly effective for first-generation college students who need reinforcement of their potential and proof that opportunities are real. The living and learning site has power to transform the students' self-esteem and to raise their aspirational levels. It is now a demonstrated program which can easily be established through academic partnerships all over the country" (Lieberman, 1989).

Conclusion

First-generation college students are becoming an increasingly significant force in higher education. They embody an inexhaustible source of talent and potential, and their motivation is fueled by a passion to improve the quality of their lives beyond what their histories would suggest. The educational programs described in this chapter represent LaGuardia's efforts to serve these students in ways that are innovative and effective and that equip students with the tools they will need to achieve their dreams.

References

Arendt, H. *The Life of the Mind.* New York: Harcourt Brace Jovanovich, 1978.

Chaffee, J. "Final Report for the National Endowment for the Humanities." Unpublished report, LaGuardia Community College, 1985.

Cullen, C. "A Review of Middle College." Unpublished report prepared for the National Demonstration Network, 1989.

Dickinson, S. "When Is a Kamoodgel Not a Kamoodgel?" In J. Chaffee (ed.), *Thinking Critically.* Boston: Houghton Mifflin, 1991.

Kirk, G. S., and Raven, J. E. *The Pre-Socratic Philosophers: A Critical History with a Selection of Texts.* Cambridge, Mass.: University Press, 1966.

Lieberman, J. E. Acceptance address for the Charles A. Dana Awards, New York, 1989.

Lieberman, J. E., and Lieberman, R. K. *City Limits.* Dubuque, Iowa: Kendall-Hunt, 1983.

Lieberman, R. K. "Family History: Learning About Your Past." In S. H. Cutcliffe (ed.), *Humanities Perspectives on Technology Program: Science, Technology, and Society Program.* Bethlehem, Pa.: Lehigh University, 1979. 302 pp. (ED 201 238)

Nissman, S. "Vassar Summer Project." Unpublished report, Vassar College, 1987.

Singer, C. "Facts Are Fine; Historical Reasoning Is Finer." *New York Times,* April 23, 1988, Section A.

Vygotsky, L. *Thought and Language.* (A. Kozulin, ed. and trans.) Cambridge, Mass.: BMIT Press, 1978.

JOHN CHAFFEE is director of critical thinking studies at LaGuardia Community College.

Today one must look to the tribally controlled colleges to find success among American Indian first-generation students.

Tribal Colleges: A Success Story

Wayne J. Stein

The advent of the tribally controlled college in the 1960s was the response of American Indian people to years of cultural, educational, and racial suppression perpetrated on them by an unrelenting dominant society. The vision of Guy Gorman of Navajo Community College, Stanley Red Bird of Sinte Gleska College, Gerald One Feather of Oglala Lakota College, David Risling of D-Q University, and many others was to regain some control for education for their people and at the same time give their students in higher education a chance to succeed. These leaders recognized that the gateway to their peoples' regaining control of their destiny was through tribally controlled education.

Today there are twenty-four tribally controlled colleges scattered from the state of Washington to Michigan and from North Dakota to Arizona. These colleges serve a wide variety of tribes, but all adhere to several basic principles in their mission statements. Each has stated clearly that the will to preserve, enhance, and promote the language and culture of its tribe is central to its existence. The colleges serve their communities through research on economic development, human resource development, and community organization. Each strives to provide quality academic programs for students seeking a two-year degree for transfer to a senior institution, and wherever possible, each provides the vocational and technical programs that help ensure that students will find decent jobs in their community on completion of the program (Carnegie Foundation for the Advancement of Teaching, 1989).

Of all the determinants that motivate the faculty, administrators, and staff in the tribal colleges, the single most important element is the students. Tribal colleges are dedicated to the success of their students. The programs developed to serve the special needs of the students, as well as individual acts of caring by tribal college administrators, faculty, and staff, amply demonstrate this dedication.

Students of the Tribally Controlled College

American Indian students who enroll at tribal colleges attend them for many of the same reasons that non-Indians attend college. They desire to better themselves intellectually, hope to improve their chances of securing good and rewarding employment, seek the skills to manage their own futures, and want the opportunity to provide a better life for their families. What makes them different from non-Indian college students is their physical and spiritual situation. Many are older (over thirty); the majority are female single heads of households; many have failed at non-Indian higher education institutions, have extended family obligations, and find college an unusually heavy burden; and virtually all are the first in their families to attend college (Boyer, 1990). Tribal college students are actively seeking proficiency in their own languages. Among Crow students, 87 percent still speak the Crow language as their first language. Traditional spiritual ceremonies and arts remain an integral part of the communities from which American Indian students come, and tribal colleges have generated great pride in the individual tribal heritages (Carnegie Foundation for the Advancement of Teaching, 1989; Boyer, 1990).

Programs and Special Services for Tribal College Students

American Indian students attending a tribal college present their instructors and counselors with many challenging cultural, linguistic, and personal situations. Tribes in the western United States have existed for the past century in abject poverty; this is reflected by tribal members who attend tribal colleges. They bring with them a value system that is a hybrid of native culture, mainstream culture, and welfare culture. Instructors and students often have to sort through this cultural mix in order to create for each student a productive and healthy plan to get through the program of the college.

Recognizing that nearly 90 percent of the students attending a tribal college are first-generation students has been a major landmark in the development of programs that enhance the chances that these students will stay in school. Each tribal college's mission statement states clearly that it will help preserve, promote, and teach its tribe's culture and language. This important goal provides the students with an opportunity to learn more about their tribe's history and culture, which in turn helps build a sense of identity and pride. These qualities are important to American Indian students as they struggle to overcome poverty, lack of self-esteem, and poor education in their quest for a higher education. The college, in turn, has to examine itself constantly to ensure that the programs it has developed are the ones that will best assist students through the college experience.

Several colleges have expanded their services to students by providing sorely needed transportation and child care. The need for these services reflects the demanding environment from which first-generation American Indian students come. The tribal colleges are located in some of the most rural and isolated parts of the United States. In addition, most Indian reservations have poor road systems with few paved highways, as well as severe weather conditions in winter and long distances between the small communities on the reservations. Many students have unreliable vehicles. Thus, even in the best weather, students often need the service of a college-sponsored transportation system.

Child care assists those students who have demands on their time and resources from children, grandchildren, or younger siblings. Tribal college students reflect their culture at its best when they take on the responsibility of child care. Unfortunately, this responsibility can lead to academic absenteeism, insufficient financial aid to cover the needs of an extended family, and lack of time to study and prepare for class. Those tribal colleges that have a child-care program have gone a long way toward helping students at a basic and necessary level.

Carol Murray (personal interview, January 8, 1991), vice president of student services at Blackfeet Community College (BCC), reports that one of the college's most important and successful new programs is the Women's Support Group. The group meets regularly after classes to discuss and develop strategies to help members cope with the burdens of filling so many demanding roles at once: student, mother, wife or single head of household, and often major provider. The Women's Support Group has become so visibly successful for the women students who participate that several of BCC's male students have approached Murray, requesting that the college sponsor a similar program for them.

Several of the more traditional student services programs deserve a closer look for their contribution to the success of first-generation students at the tribal colleges. These programs illustrate how important a wide variety of counseling and service programs are to these students.

Most tribal colleges place importance on the adult basic education (ABE) programs (also known as graduate equivalency degree, or GED, programs) because of the substantial number of their student recruits who lack a high school diploma. The tribal colleges' ABE programs have become a significant part of the reservation educational scene as an alarming 55 percent of American Indian students drop out of junior and senior high school.

At the Montana Pipeline Conference, held at Montana State University in May 1990 and sponsored by the Montana Committee for American

Indian Higher Education, Lionel Bordeaux (1990), president of Sinte Gleska College in Rosebud, South Dakota, told of how important and effective a well-run tribal college ABE program can be. Sinte Gleska has graduated more than 1,000 Rosebud Indian students from its ABE program over the past ten years, in contrast to the fewer than 100 graduates from the earlier program run by the state of South Dakota throughout several decades.

The June 1989 graduation ceremonies of Blackfeet Community College in Browning, Montana, also demonstrated the importance of ABE programs. There were as many GED graduates as there were recipients of certificates or two-year degrees.

Tribal College Personnel

The success of programs in the tribal colleges naturally depends on the people who administer and teach there. The teachers, administrators, and board members of the tribal colleges are a unique group of individuals within the higher education community. They come to the tribal colleges with mixed backgrounds: they include those who are American Indian and those who are not; some have a great deal of education, and some have little; and they come from both urban and rural environments. The ingredient that holds this unique group together is a dedication to the success of their American Indian students. This dedication is expressed by the time, effort, and creativity with which they discharge their responsibilities to the students of the tribal colleges.

Board members have provided the glue that holds the tribal colleges together. They are community members who have decided that their people must have the opportunity to succeed and that in order to do so, they must have a locally controlled higher education institution to attend. Because board members come from the tribal community themselves, they understand the difficulties facing the first-generation American Indian student who chooses to attend college. Thus, board members seek out administrators and teachers who will put the needs of their students first and will base decisions that affect the future of the college on those needs.

The administrators of the tribal colleges use their positions to actualize the dreams of their boards of trustees. Most tribal college administrators also teach, advise, or mentor students on a regular basis. It is common for deans of students and occasionally for presidents of tribal colleges to go to students' homes to find out why a student has been missing class (Patricia Stump, personal interview, December 6, 1990). This concern for the individual student has played an important role in the high retention rates of first-generation American Indian students within the tribal colleges.

Retention rates for the tribal colleges can be measured in two ways:

through the conventional fashion, which counts as a dropout any student who leaves college before completion of a degree program, in which case tribal colleges have a retention rate of approximately 45 percent; or through a more accurate method, used by the tribal colleges, which labels as "stop-outs" those who leave and then return within a quarter to continue their studies. By measuring in this fashion, the colleges' retention rate is approximately 75 to 80 percent. Students who stop out generally do so because of financial difficulties or because they have been put on academic probation (Avis Three Irons, personal interview, Jan. 1991).

Further results of tribal colleges' special interest in the individual student can be found in research done by the American Indian Higher Education Consortium (AIHEC) for testimony in 1983 before appropriations committees of the U.S. Congress. AIHEC found that American Indian students who completed a course of study at a tribal college went on to complete a four-year degree program at a senior institution with a 75 percent greater success rate than American Indian students who bypassed tribal colleges and went directly to four-year institutions. Another interesting finding of the AIHEC survey was that about 85 percent of tribal college graduates who stayed on the reservation were employed—a significant fact on reservations, which have from 45 to 80 percent unemployment rates (American Indian Higher Education Consortium, 1983).

Like the administrators, teachers have played a significant role in the success of tribal colleges in serving their first-generation students. They provide the front-line, daily contact with the students, and this contact often dictates how well a student will do over the course of a year. Besides providing instruction to students, the teachers must often touch their students in a personal way. Gerald Wagner (personal interview, December 7, 1990), a Montana State University senior, reports that while he was attending Little Big Horn Community College at Crow Agency, Montana, he received personalized instruction from teachers who were committed to giving him a strong science base so that he could qualify for the biomedical research program for American Indian students at Montana State University. This dedication and caring extended so far that when he lost his means of transportation between Little Big Horn College and his home community some twelve miles away, a teacher made it a point to transport him to and from school each day.

Conrad Fisher (personal interview, December 6, 1990), another first-generation tribal college student now studying at Montana State University, received his university preparation at Dull Knife Memorial College (DKMC) in Lame Deer, Montana. He states that without the encouragement and personalized instruction he received outside of regularly scheduled classes, he would not have been prepared for the more rigorous third- and fourth-year classes he encountered at Montana State University.

Teachers at DKMC spent extra time at least one day a week helping him with the math assignments he found difficult until he had mastered the material.

Carol Michell (personal interview, December 6, 1990), a former student at Blackfeet Community College (BCC) in Browning, Montana, who is now studying at Montana State University, states that teachers both gave her strong encouragement and also made her work hard. One instructor was constantly criticized by Michell's fellow students for demanding so much of them, but she now realizes that he was preparing them for success at a senior institution by making them face reality at the tribal college. She understands that once on the campus of a large institution, the personalized instruction she received at BCC is much rarer and that a student is expected to work independently.

Linda Iron (personal interview, December 5, 1990), dean of academics at Standing Rock College (SRC) in Fort Yates, North Dakota, explains that teachers at SRC require students to keep a journal of their activities. Students are also required to write their own obituaries up to that point in their lives. She says that the two activities force students to examine their personal histories and to reflect on what occurs in their daily lives that affects their abilities as students. For most American Indian students, this self-appraisal can be a jolting experience. Often it is the first time they have examined the past with an eye on the future. Teachers then use these insights to advise and guide their students through the curriculum with the goal of fulfilling the students' dreams for the future.

Most first-generation American Indian students welcome the attention of the administrators, teachers, and support staff of the tribal colleges. Often the students are faced with indifference and even hostility from their families and peers once they decide to attend college. Dean Patty Stump of Fort Peck Community College reveals that many of her students must overcome hostile home environments to attend college. Family members who did not go to college often seem to devalue education or are threatened when a spouse or sibling decides to pursue a college education.

This lack of support for first-generation Indian students can be explained by looking at American Indian culture. One of its strongest principles, found in almost every tribe, is that of putting the interests or welfare of the family and tribe ahead of any individual's desires or needs. When a family member or close friend decides to embark on a path that will take that person out of the familiar circle of the family or peer group, this change is often seen as a form of desertion and can lead to accusations of putting the self ahead of the group. American Indian students often face this kind of questioning when they decide to attend college. If they succeed at school, the criticism can intensify. College personnel must be aware of this and be prepared to help their students deal with the internal conflicts it engenders.

It has also been said by a number of American Indians that their people have taken on some of the distorted views of themselves held by the dominant non-Indian culture that surrounds them. Thus, many doubt their own or any Indian's intelligence or capacity to succeed in higher education. These doubts must be understood and overcome if first-generation Indian students are to succeed.

Whether the level of encouragement from family or friends is high or low, the tribal colleges provide support on which first-generation American Indian students can build their educational futures. The tribal colleges provide student support groups, individual counseling, and community education. The effort to educate the communities from which the first-generation American Indian students come may prove to be the most successful intervention method employed by the colleges. The evidence of this is the pride that Indian communities now have in their colleges.

Conclusion

Tribal colleges are successful at the twenty-four sites where they have grown and flourished. This success has varied from college to college, and not every tribal college started has survived. Several have had to close their doors, which is not uncommon among higher education institutions in the United States. Where tribal colleges have succeeded, however, first-generation American Indian students are making strides academically and are having a positive impact on their communities. Many Indian people see the tribal colleges as the embodiment of American Indian self-determination and the best means for regaining some measure of control over their lives.

Though the tribal college movement has slowed its expansion across the Indian reservations of the United States, every few years a new tribal college opens its doors, and the quality of educational programs at these institutions continues to improve. The number of American Indian students attending tribal colleges grows substantially each year. The tribal college is the most effective institution for launching first-generation American Indian students on the successful pursuit of higher education.

References

American Indian Higher Education Consortium. Testimony to the Senate and House Appropriations Committee, Washington, D.C., March 1983.

Bordeaux, L. "Higher Education from the Tribal College Perspective." Paper presented at the Montana Pipeline Conference, Bozeman, Montana, May 1990.

Boyer, P. "Tribal Colleges: Creating a New Partnership in Higher Education." Paper presented at the Montana Pipeline Conference, Bozeman, Montana, May 1990.

Carnegie Foundation for the Advancement of Teaching. *Tribal Colleges: Shaping the Future of Native America.* Lawrenceville, N.J.: Princeton University Press, 1989. 111 pp. (ED 311 990)

WAYNE J. STEIN is director of the Office of Tribal Service, Center for Native American Studies, and is assistant professor of higher education at Montana State University. He is a former president of a tribal college.

Qualitative research reveals ways in which Asian immigrant and refugee students view their college experience. Popular images of these students are invalidated, and urban institutions are challenged to recognize their growing presence.

Issues of Curriculum and Community for First-Generation Asian Americans in College

Peter Nien-chu Kiang

Since the liberalization of U.S. immigration laws less than three decades ago, major shifts have occurred in the Asian American landscape. The growth and diversification of the Asian American population resulting from sustained immigration since 1965 and Southeast Asian refugee resettlement since 1975 have been phenomenal. Koreatowns, Little Saigons, and new Chinatown communities have emerged as the Asian American population has become predominantly foreign born (Barringer, 1991; Gardner, Robey, and Smith, 1985; O'Hare and Felt, 1991).

The Asian American student population, from preschool to graduate school, has also grown dramatically during this period, driven by demographic changes and fueled by socioeconomic pressures and cultural priorities. Department of Education data show that Asian American college enrollments jumped by more than 110 percent nationally between 1978 and 1988. In contrast, Hispanic college student enrollments increased by 63 percent, while white student enrollments rose by 12 percent and African American college enrollments grew by 7 percent during the same period. Asian Americans, including Koreans, Japanese, Chinese, Vietnamese, Lao, and Cambodians, have emerged (along with Filipinos, South Asians, and Southeast Asians) as the largest minority student group at many schools today (Hsia and Hirano-Nakanishi, 1989; Morgan and Mercer, 1990; Nagasawa and Espinosa, 1992).

Asian American college students are often portrayed as superachieving whiz kids who are taking over the country's most selective private universities, such as Harvard, Stanford, and the Massachusetts Institute of Technology (Brand, 1987; Butterfield, 1990). In fact, less than 20 percent of all Asian American students in college go to private four-year schools. Eighty-two percent attend public institutions, and 40 percent of all Asian Americans enrolled in higher education institutions attend two-year community colleges (U.S. Department of Education, 1990).

Most research on Asian Americans in higher education has either aggregated data from various nationalities under one umbrella category or focused on Chinese and Japanese Americans—the Asian nationalities with the longest histories in the United States. Only a handful of studies have examined the experiences of recent immigrants and refugees such as Vietnamese, Cambodian, or Lao college students in public universities and community colleges (Fernandez, 1988; Kiang, 1990a, 1990b, 1991; Nguyen and Halpern, 1989; Nguyen, 1988; Skinner and Hendricks, 1979).

However, as the demands of a rapidly growing and diversifying Asian American student population make themselves increasingly felt, college administrators, faculty, and staff, as well as students, must confront important questions regarding admissions policies, support service delivery, faculty and staff representation, curricular reforms, and community relations. This chapter draws from a larger qualitative study (Kiang, 1991) on how first-generation Asian immigrant and refugee students view and shape their college experience at an urban public university in the northeastern United States.

Institutional Context and Issues of Student Persistence

The site of this study is an urban public university that serves as the only relatively affordable four-year college in the metropolitan area. Students attending the university share similar cultural and socioeconomic profiles as well as academic backgrounds with local community college students. Each year, 20 percent of the university's new student enrollment is comprised of transfers from the area's community colleges. The university functions as the main bridge to education beyond the two-year community colleges for many recent immigrant and refugee students.

The university is located in a neighborhood where the Asian American population grew more than 730 percent during the 1980s. The Asian student population at the university has more than tripled since 1980. About 10 percent of the entering class in 1990 was Asian American (excluding nonresident aliens). The university enrolls the highest percentage of Southeast Asian students of any four-year college or university in the region. However, institutional data show that Asians, along with Hispanics and blacks, have significantly lower retention and graduation rates than white students (Office of Policy Research and Planning, 1989a). Less than

14 percent of the Asian students who entered in 1981 and 1982, for example, had graduated at the end of five years.

Lee's (1987) survey of the university's Asian American student population observed that 66 percent of the respondents had been in the U.S. for six years or less. Eighty percent were more comfortable using their native Asian language than they were using English. Only 6 percent of the sample were American born. Nearly 80 percent of the sample worked, in addition to going to school full time, with six out of ten respondents working more than sixteen hours each week. This profile is also typical of many Asian students attending the local community colleges.

Lee noted that 56 percent of the sample were majoring in business, engineering, computer science, or natural science. Fifteen percent were majoring in social science, 10 percent majored in "other," and 19 percent were undeclared. Lee's findings are supported by institutional data (Office of Policy Research and Planning, 1989b, 1990) that show that 75 percent of the Asian undergraduates in 1989 were majoring in math, natural sciences, and management or were undeclared. The meaning and significance of these choices of majors are discussed in a later section.

The high percentage of undeclared majors—19 percent in Lee's study and 37 percent according to institutional data—may be related to another of Lee's findings that half of the sample reported not utilizing any of the university's existing support services, including career services, counseling, tutoring, and academic advising. Sample interviewees reported that they relied primarily on friendship networks with other Asian students for assistance in negotiating their university experience. Respondents were significantly more likely to use each category of support services, however, if bilingual, bicultural personnel were available.

Research on student attrition and retention (Ramist, 1981; Tinto, 1975, 1987) has recommended early and systematic institutional intervention to enhance the persistence of students in college. In describing his model of student attrition, Tinto (1987) notes, "Persistence entails the incorporation, that is integration, of the individual as a competent member in the social and intellectual communities of the college. In this regard, colleges are viewed as being made up of a range of communities whose interactional attributes have much to do with the eventual leaving of many of their students. Student institutional departure is as much a reflection of the attributes of those communities, and therefore of the institution, as it is of the students who enter that institution" (pp. 126–127).

Most research on college student attrition and retention has utilized quantitative research designs (Astin, 1975, 1977; Stage, 1990). Qualitative research, however, can complement quantitative studies by uncovering, for example, the perspectives, decision-making processes, and survival strategies developed by students to stay in or depart from school (Attinasi,

1989). The following themes emerge from qualitative research on how Asian immigrant and refugee students view and shape the meaning of their college experience at an urban public university (Kiang, 1990b, 1991). The informants for these studies were Vietnamese, Cambodian, and Chinese— representing the predominant Asian nationalities enrolled in the university. There are no Hmong and less than five Lao enrolled currently. In any study of Asian Americans, it is critical to recognize differences as well as commonalities among the disaggregated sample and with other Asian ethnic groups who are not included in the study. In the following sections, quotations are verbatim from interview transcripts.

Success Entails a Struggle for Survival

> It was very hard to come to a new land . . . I thought that I came from another planet. I became homesick and depressed. I stayed inside the house all the time. . . . Even though today I speak English, I still have to repeat and repeat so that American people understand me.

Although images of spelling-bee champions and Westinghouse Science competition winners represent the dominant portrayal of Asian American students, even a superficial glance at the experience of immigrant and refugee students reveals a reality of struggle and survival rather than success and academic achievement.

Because of the language barrier, many students experience greater difficulty and frustration in both academic and social domains than do native English-speaking students. Academically, for example, a Cambodian student states:

> When you talk, people kind of look at you and say, "You've got a funny pronunciation," you know, funny accent. And you don't speak English the way, you know, a West European or American speaks. And it's just, I feel shy, you know. Kind of lost. 'Cause you don't want to say anything. You have the answer professor asks, you know. Most of the time, they ask questions, they say, raise your hand. You don't want to raise your hand. You know the answer, what the answer is, but you don't want to say it.

While speaking up in class presents one set of obstacles for immigrant and refugee students, the task of taking comprehensive notes of lectures, discussions, and reviews of readings presents another. As a Cambodian student sighs, "They're talking about all these terminology you never heard before. . . . And in your country you never heard of this stuff. . . . You look it up in bilingual dictionary—they have no name." The burden is compounded outside of the classroom, too. A reading assignment that an

American-born Asian student completes in just one hour, for example, might take an immigrant or refugee student more than four hours to finish.

The experience of isolation affects students socially as well as academically. A Vietnamese student observes:

> When I came here, I don't have many friends, and I don't feel free to speak in American class, and I don't have a lot of American friends. I don't know their history or maybe the culture or anything. We don't talk together a lot. And actually, until today, I have been here for five years, but I don't have any close friends who we can have a talk like friends.

Unlike many international students who may share similar difficulties with the language barrier, most immigrant and refugee students are working class and may spend fifteen to fifty hours working each week. Many ethnic Chinese and Vietnamese students, for example, have work-study jobs in offices on campus during the week and work in restaurants on the weekends. In many cases, they also experience discrimination on the job from employers who assign them extra work without extra compensation and from customers who harass them with racial slurs. For example, a Cambodian student working as a grocery store cashier was told, "Why don't you go back to your country?" The physical and emotional demands of work, therefore, further reduce both the quantity and quality of time available for school.

Furthermore, immigrant and refugee students carry the weight of many family pressures. In most cases, these Asian students are the first generation in their families to go to college in the United States. Many also have family members still living in their home countries. The dangers and difficulties they have survived in leaving their homelands and the hopes and dreams for a better life that they bring to this country all become concentrated in family expectations that this generation will go to college and do well.

When these students falter in school, then, they must deal not only with their own disappointment but also with the added sense that they are failing their families. A student who was academically suspended from school but did not inform his parents in Vietnam laments, "I haven't sent any letter to them. . . . I hate myself, and I hate everything. That's why I don't want to, I don't want them to know what I did here because I didn't do what they want me, expect me to be."

These students also have major responsibilities within their families, especially in serving as the interpreters and intermediaries between their parents and American society. A Chinese Cambodian student describes his duties as "Translate problems and reading English, writing . . . go to hospital, pay the bill, writing letter, making phone calls. Communicating with outside. And also I worked to support my family, help pay rent."

In these ways, immigrant and refugee students play critical roles in enabling their families to survive in this country. Though many may wish to achieve some degree of independence from their families, they feel that they have no alternative. A Chinese Vietnamese student sighs, "We children in America are like decision maker in family. . . . I feel pain in neck sometimes doing this much work. . . . We become responsible." Though she dreams of getting her own apartment, a Vietnamese student whose parents recently arrived from Vietnam admits that she feels obligated to take care of them in this country and that they would never understand if she moved out.

Added to their difficulties with school, work, and family life, immigrant and refugee students also face the realities of being urban minorities in a racist society. As is well documented, the 1980s witnessed a dramatic rise in anti-Asian violence around the country (Asian American Resource Workshop, 1987; Japanese American Citizens' League, 1985; U.S. Commission on Civil Rights, 1987). Growing reports of racial violence and harassment on campus have also caused widespread alarm in recent years (Kagiwada, 1989; McClelland, 1990; Morse, 1989). Suzuki (1989) suggests that the social and psychological problems of Asian students may be increasing because of the climate of growing anti-Asian sentiment and the increase in racial violence on campus. In addition to documenting stabbings and assaults, Suzuki notes that "more subtle forms of discrimination can include such incidents as derogatory remarks by instructors about the limited English proficiency of Asian immigrant students, subtly racist statements about Asians by both instructors and students, or expressions of resentment by other students toward the achievement orientation of Asian students. Such incidents can inflict serious psychological damage on Asian students, affecting their social adjustment to campus as well as their academic performance" (p. 25).

Clearly, the obstacles, barriers, and constraints faced by refugee and immigrant students turn every day into a struggle for survival. Although discredited by many schools (Chun, 1980; Hsia, 1988; Suzuki, 1977, 1989), the stereotype of Asian American students as superachieving whiz kids nevertheless continues to define them on campus and hides the reality of sacrifice that characterizes daily life for so many. Thus, the lack of institutionalized support for Asian American students can be justified by the myth that they "have no problems." Furthermore, this stereotype sets an unfair standard that many immigrant and refugee students will never be able to meet simply because of the concrete conditions of their daily lives.

Even at community colleges where there is typically greater emphasis on providing support services for "nontraditional" students, these dynamics, combined with cultural differences regarding service utilization, may still leave first-generation Asian students' needs unrecognized or underserved. For example, Atkinson, Ponterotto, and Sanchez (1984) find significant differences between Vietnamese and Anglo-American student attitudes toward counseling at a community college. When asked to rank to whom they would go for help in discussing a personal problem, both Vietnamese and Anglo-American students picked friends as their first choice. The Vietnamese students chose an older relative second and the oldest person in the community third. In contrast, the Anglo-American students chose a psychologist-counselor second and an older relative third. The oldest person in the community was the seventh and least desirable choice for the Anglo-American students. Atkinson, Ponterotto, and Sanchez recommend that "counseling centers located in colleges that enroll Vietnamese students may want to encourage the development of support groups within the Vietnamese student community. As their data indicate, the age range of Vietnamese students enrolled in community colleges includes middle-aged persons. By encouraging the development of Vietnamese student support systems, particularly those in which older students can help younger students with their personal problems, counseling centers may be able to make use of a mental health paradigm indigenous to the Vietnamese culture" (p. 452).

Issues of Identity and Alienation

> I'm happier here in a way because I can look for a better future. But in spirit, no. In Cambodia, I would feel shoulder to shoulder with the people. Even if I were a farmer, I would be proud; I would be qualified. Here, I feel so bad spiritually.

Asian immigrant and refugee students share a multiplicity of needs as well as a range of strengths that reflect various dimensions of their historical and cultural backgrounds, their individual identities, and their social realities. These background characteristics can be defined along four dimensions (Kiang, 1990a, 1991):

As *Southeast Asians* with distinct linguistic, cultural, and historical characteristics determined by growing up in their home countries and, to some extent, maintained by their continuing integration in their basic family and community structure in the United States

As *refugees* with survival skills and psychologies adapted to war, famine, flight and forced migration, loss of family members, secondary trauma from refugee camps, and resettlement

As *new immigrants* in America adjusting to drastic changes in status, opportunity, daily life and living conditions, climate, and especially culture and language

As *racial minorities* facing discrimination, disenfranchisement, and racism as social, economic, and political realities in the United States.

Considered individually, each dimension uncovers specific issues faced by Southeast Asian college students and points to specific directions for further study. Considered together, these elements provide a multidimensional framework for analyzing the literature on Southeast Asian college students in an integrated manner. In practice, however, if trained bilingual, bicultural staff and targeted services are not provided, the difficulties of survival and adjustment faced by immigrant and refugee students often go unrecognized and unanswered.

A Chinese Vietnamese student recalls, "I remember a lot of students in my time when I was in college for the first and second years, a lot of students dropped out because they don't know where to go. . . . And at that time, there was nobody to help them. And they kind of feel disappointed and depressed when they get a bad grade. That's why they can't stay on the campus no more and they dropped out."

The lack of appropriate campus-based services adds to the already central role of faculty who are traditionally entrusted by Asian immigrant and refugee families with full authority to guide young people in their learning (Henkin and Nguyen, 1981; Nguyen, 1984). To understand and improve the college experience of first-generation Asian immigrant and refugee students, therefore, we must examine the role of teaching and the curriculum.

Lessons from the Classroom

I learned so many things I had never known before . . . to know the history of Asians in America which I think I will not learn from history books. This course is really interesting to me, maybe because the course is about Asians. In this class, I did not feel left out unlike other classes.

Although the university had a well-established English-as-a-second-language program and academic advising services in place to address the needs of the Asian student population, there was little else in the curriculum that recognized their growing presence until 1988, when a cluster of three Asian American Studies courses was developed. Since then, the courses have provided an important context within the university that enables Asian students to feel integrated academically and socially. Kiang (1989) and Hune (1989) address the value of Asian American Studies curricula for first-generation students.

The three courses include an introduction to Asian American history and contemporary issues, a survey of the Southeast Asian refugee experience, and a research seminar on community issues. Through the courses, students develop a historical and social analysis of the Asian American experience that they are then able to apply to their own lives. This helps students realize that the problems they face are largely not of their own making. With a clear analysis, they have the capacity to address many of these problems more effectively and also to understand why some cannot be solved by their own individual efforts. The kinds of problem-solving skills they learn include, for example, how to manage cultural conflicts that arise between the generations in the family; what factors, including quality-of-life concerns, should be considered in making decisions about one's education and career; and how to build conscious support systems. Communication is also emphasized and supported by the courses' learning environment, enabling students to find their voices and develop the strength to speak up.

Many immigrant students comment that they always feel self-conscious about their accents and poor command of English in other courses. When they try to participate, their teachers make them repeat themselves or don't take their points seriously, so they choose to withdraw instead. In the Asian American studies classes, however, they report feeling a higher level of respect in the classroom, and they begin to participate and learn more actively as a result. A Cambodian student describes the difference in terms of death and life, concepts with which he is intimately familiar: "You go to another course, sit back, and, you know, just write down notes. And then when you get out of that class, go to another one, same thing. Next day, before you come to your class, you go another class, like you're dead. And then, all of a sudden [in the Asian American Studies classes], you come alive, you know. Full of life!"

The supportive learning environment also has to do with teaching practices that are appropriate to students whose first language is not English. Immigrant students appreciate having as much information as possible written on the board. Videotapes help to illustrate lectures and facilitate discussion in class. Students respond more readily to such challenges as making oral presentations on their final projects because the classroom atmosphere is encouraging and everyone is going through it together. There is no reason to be self-conscious about one's accent because everyone has one. A Chinese Vietnamese student notes, "The majority of the class was Asian students. There were not many native white students in the class. So we kind of have the same kind of feeling in this country and same kind of cultures. . . . So we kind of confident to speak out, even though we are not yet good in English or maybe even though we speak the wrong grammar or the wrong sentences, they still understand what we are trying to say."

Interestingly, these efforts to enable Asian students to participate comfortably in the classroom also effectively reach students of other backgrounds, particularly working-class, immigrant, and minority students, older students, and veterans who comprise large segments of the university's student body and who typically represent the profiles of students enrolled in community colleges. Many Vietnam veterans, for example, are returning to college for the first time in twenty years and feel anxious about their skills and learning abilities. Like the Asian students, they appreciate pedagogical strategies that facilitate a supportive learning environment. Veterans and refugees taking Asian American Studies courses are able to work together in the classroom in a way that rarely occurs in the society at large, and through these experiences, they can recognize both their shared histories in Southeast Asia and their shared destinies in this country.

Reflections on Gender

It's time for Vietnamese to ask for equal rights and good opportunities for our first generation. Vietnamese women should be ready and involved in political community work and encourage men to go on. If men hold back or don't want to walk forward, women should strongly lead the community.

Gender also seems to be a major determining factor in immigrant and refugee students' experiences. While many immigrant and refugee men look back nostalgically at their former lives of relative status and dominance within the family and traditional society, they bitterly and perhaps correctly view their coming to the United States as a loss of options and opportunities. Prior to immigration, most men were their families' sole breadwinners; here, their minimum-wage earnings in the local service industry are not sufficient to meet the needs of their families. Their attention emotionally and politically focuses typically on the past and future of their homeland, with only minimal engagement in the affairs of American society.

In contrast to traditional expectations in their home countries, women face a socioeconomic reality here that places them in school and work out of necessity. In these settings, however, they develop new views of their individual capabilities and social potential. Coming to the United States provides opportunities that would not have been available to them had their traditional social roles been maintained. They tend to become more quickly and fully engaged in the affairs of American society and, in the process, become more critical of American institutions and social policies.

A Cambodian male student explains with some ambivalence, "Women change faster than men. . . . I don't know, like men, because they don't want to change anything, they like the way it is. But women, they want to change because they want the equality, they want the freedom, they want to be independent. They want to show men how strong they are. They want to be aggressive. Right now in the Cambodian community, girls seem to be more succeed [successful] than men. A lot of girls stay in college."

A Cambodian female student adds, "Since I am a woman, you know, my people tend to think that women cannot do anything as good as men. So, by having a degree to prove it, that I have achieved, then probably they take me a little bit seriously."

This process of change in gender roles and expectations has implications for the future, as increasing numbers of women will see themselves playing significant roles in their communities but will have to face traditional norms and a male-dominated community leadership. There is also evidence to suggest that young women, particularly in the Cambodian and Hmong communities, also leave school in large numbers to marry according to traditional familial and cultural expectations (Goldstein, 1988; Vang, 1991).

"Major Stories" and Visions of the Next Generation

> I hope that I have a brighter future over here because I can go to school and get a good education. I study hard so that later I can get a good job to support my parents and take care of them in their old age. I will use my study to serve, to work for the Asian American community.

In addition to the direct impact of these courses on students in the classroom, there are long-term implications of the Asian American Studies curriculum for both individuals and the community. As institutional data (Office of Policy Research and Planning, 1990) and Lee's (1987) study both show, a majority of Asian immigrant and refugee students are concentrated in a relatively narrow selection of majors, including business, engineering, and computer sciences.

The reasons for this narrow concentration of majors are easy to explain. First, technical fields require relatively few verbal and written English language skills; thus, they are especially attractive to immigrant students. A Cambodian student who transferred to the university from a community college recalls, "The first time semester I was here, I gone through a lot of hard times. I could not manage many courses. I got depressed. I cry many times that I could not make it. Professors or some of my friends could not help me. Yeah, I walk out from classes and cry, probably I could not make it. And never think I would graduate, but just take one day at a time, learn. And very frustrated because do not have any help from the school. So, just thinking that the English, I cannot do it, you know. Many courses that I had, just too hard. So I just took math courses."

Second, beginning as early as elementary school, students are tracked by teachers, guidance counselors, and even friends who stereotypically assume that Asians are good at math and science but not so good in arts and letters. Meanwhile, parents also exert tremendous pressure, expecting their children to select career paths with professional status or at least a financial return.

Third, the criteria used for evaluation in the technical fields tend to be objective. Individual interpretation and subjective evaluation, whether based on personality, cultural differences, or racial bias, are less influential in the sciences and technical fields. Therefore, the chance for discrimination is perceived to be less.

Thus, many Asian students may not be personally interested in engineering or computers but may feel that they have no other viable options. Paula Bagasao (1989) coined the term "major stories" to refer to the conflicts experienced by Asian American students who typically choose and change majors within scientific and technical fields because they feel they have no choice. Many Asian students have major stories to tell. A Chinese Vietnamese economics major explains, "We can't rely on whatever the major we're interested in, but we have to go from [for] the major whichever is easiest for us to accomplish."

Hsia (1988) argues that while concentrating in scientific and technical fields may be a viable survival strategy for Asian American students in school, it may also retard their intellectual and social development in other critical areas such as English language acquisition and social integration. A Vietnamese accounting major agrees: "Most Vietnamese students, they choose computers or engineering as their major because they was afraid to read; I mean basically in the math, you can study engineering or computers. So they took it because they try to avoid the problem, their English problem, I guess. So even when some students they graduated from engineering, they didn't talk much and sometimes they didn't understand what that means, I mean the simple words. . . . But they didn't know, I mean, which majors, which way is better for them. . . . And they didn't care as far [long] as they graduated."

However, some students who have taken Asian American Studies are shifting their priorities. Students have changed majors from management to education, hoping to become elementary school teachers. Others have left computer science, nursing, and biology in order to pursue photojournalism, social work, and law. Asian American Studies helps to widen the range of possible majors and future career alternatives that are accessible and meaningful to Asian students. Social science disciplines like sociology, history, and psychology are useful and interesting when analyzing the struggles of one's community. Literature, poetry, and photography are relevant and powerful when expressing the hopes and dreams of one's heritage. A Vietnamese student recalls, "I think those years were frustrated, just took the courses and that's all . . . and then I think it really big change . . . so I decide to be in sociology. And then after that, I have a clear direction. I can do things. I can graduate. . . . I can work in the Asian community, so that give me more, give me a clear idea."

A Cambodian student who came to the university after receiving her graduate equivalency degree from a local community college agrees: "Even when I was here two years, I still did not know what I really want, did not know what I'm good in. It's confused. . . . [When I] took the Asian Studies and sociology course, then it's like a light come in to define what really I am and what I want. . . . After that, it [my education] improved. You know, I took something that I enjoy and that I learn. Also, besides those courses, I then declare my major as sociology, and then I learn about family, about society. . . . Those courses prepare me or educate me for life which I did not know and to see how society is structured and operates."

Her sense of the course impact seems even more meaningful in light of a poignant essay she wrote at the beginning of her second year in the university before taking the course: "The more I absorb the environment I live in, the more I have a better sense of real life. I continue to see things that divide me from American society. But I could not recognize what it is and why? Everyday living just puts a lot of pressure on me, the anger and struggle I am facing are never overcome. It is crying inside me. No one wants to hear or even cares, and I have no one to turn to."

By enabling students to make better-informed decisions about their majors and future careers, universities can help to minimize the waste of human potential that results from Asian immigrants pursuing studies in which they are not really interested but that they see as their only alternatives. Taken a step further, the shift in majors and career plans observed among immigrant and refugee students in Asian American Studies classes has even more significant implications for the future development of their communities. What are the social consequences, for example, if these students concentrate overwhelmingly in business, science, and engineering when the communities, in fact, desperately need bilingual lawyers, health care providers, policymakers, writers, filmmakers, teachers, and organizers? Significantly, futures in these areas of need are more likely considered by students who have taken Asian American Studies courses. There are now four times as many Asian students majoring in sociology, for example, as there were four years ago before the Asian American courses were offered. Other evidence suggests that similar trends are emerging at other colleges (Parmley, 1990).

Directions for Further Research and Conclusions

Research on Asian immigrant and refugee college students addresses the need to focus on nontraditional and high-risk populations (Stage, 1990; Jones and Watson, 1990). Such research is useful for practitioners, policymakers, and researchers at institutions with growing numbers of Asian students, and it also addresses larger issues of student persistence at urban, commuter colleges where student retention is least likely (Morishita, 1983; Tinto, 1987). In addition, this research contributes to the knowledge base of Asian students and their families—many of whom are deeply concerned about the future of this generation in U.S. schools—and of the organizations and agencies that serve the new Asian immigrant and refugee communities.

Further research is needed to examine how first-generation Asian students define the problems they face in college. What are their survival strategies? How do they perceive their academic and social integration within the university? What role does the college experience play in enabling them to understand and resolve the complex contexts and multiple dimensions of their own identities? Studies examining these kinds of questions require analysis not only of the students' backgrounds and outlooks but also of their interrelationships with other students, faculty, and staff and with the college environment as a whole, particularly in the classroom. For example, how do cultural differences, the language barrier, and racial stereotypes affect the classroom experience and resulting social and intellectual development of Asian students?

The findings presented here indicate that the college experience of Asian immigrant and refugee students at an urban public university is characterized by struggle and survival rather than success, by complex and multifaceted issues of identity and alienation, and by changing relations and gender roles. These findings should also be applicable for community colleges that enroll and guide comparable first-generation Asian students in ever-growing numbers.

Faculty and staff at community colleges and urban universities must respond urgently and effectively to the unmet and heretofore unrecognized needs of Asian immigrant and refugee student populations. In particular, curricular reform and implementation of Asian American Studies programs may provide the much-needed content and a supportive learning environment that will enable first-generation Asian students to establish new roots and develop new voices so that they, in turn, may transform both themselves and their college experience.

References

Asian American Resource Workshop. "To Live in Peace: Responding to Anti-Asian Violence in Boston." Boston: Asian American Resource Workshop, 1987.

Astin, A. W. *Preventing Students from Dropping Out.* San Francisco: Jossey-Bass, 1975.

Astin, A. W. *Four Critical Years: Effects of College on Beliefs, Attitudes, and Knowledge.* San Francisco: Jossey-Bass, 1977.

Atkinson, D. R., Ponterotto, J. G., and Sanchez, A. R. "Attitudes of Vietnamese and Anglo-American Students Toward Counseling." *Journal of College Student Personnel,* 1984, 25 (5), 448–452.

Attinasi, L. C. "Getting In: Mexican Americans' Perceptions of University Attendance and the Implications for Freshman-Year Persistence." *Journal of Higher Education,* 1989, 60 (3), 247–277.

Bagasao, P. "Student Voices Breaking the Silence: The Asian and Pacific American Experience." *Change,* Nov.-Dec. 1989, 28–37.

Barringer, F. "Immigration Brings New Diversity to Asian Population in the U.S." *New York Times,* June 12, 1991, pp. 1, 9.

Brand, D. "The New Whiz Kids." *Time,* August 31, 1987, pp. 42–46, 49, 51.

Butterfield, F. "Why Do Asians Excel in School?" *Parade Magazine,* January 21, 1990, pp. 4–6.

Chun, K. "The Myth of Asian American Success and Its Educational Ramifications." *IRCD Bulletin,* 1980, *15* (1–2), 1–12. (ED 193 411)

Chun, K. T., and Zalokar, N. *Civil Rights Issues Facing Asian Americans in the 1990s.* Washington, D.C.: Commission on Civil Rights, 1992. 245 pp. (ED 343 979)

Fernandez, M. S. "Issues in Counseling Southeast Asian Students." *Journal of Multicultural Counseling and Development,* 1988, *16* (4), 157–166.

Gardner, R. W., Robey, B., and Smith, P. C. "Asian Americans: Growth, Change, and Diversity." *Population Bulletin,* 1985, *40* (entire issue 4). (ED 317 464)

Goldstein, B. "In Search of Survival: The Education and Integration of Hmong Refugee Girls." *Journal of Ethnic Studies,* 1988, *16* (2), 1–27.

Henkin, A. B., and Nguyen, L. T. *Between Two Cultures: The Vietnamese in America.* Saratoga, Calif.: R&E Publishers, 1981.

Hsia, J. *Asian Americans in Higher Education and at Work.* Hillsdale, N.J.: Erlbaum, 1988.

Hsia, J., and Hirano-Nakanishi, M. "The Demographics of Diversity." *Change,* Nov.-Dec. 1989, pp. 20–27.

Hune, S. "Opening the American Mind and Body: The Role of Asian American Studies." *Change,* Nov.-Dec. 1989, pp. 56–63.

Japanese American Citizens' League. "A Report on Anti-Asian Violence in the United States." San Francisco: Japanese American Citizens' League, 1985.

Jones, D. J., and Watson, B. C. " 'High-Risk' Students and Higher Education: Future Trends." Washington, D.C.: ERIC Clearinghouse on Higher Education, 1990. (ED 325 033)

Kagiwada, G. "The Killing of Thong Hy Huynh: Implications of a Rashomon Perspective." In G. M. Nomura, R. Endo, S. H. Sumida, and R. C. Leong (eds.), *Frontiers of Asian American Studies Writing, Research, and Commentary.* Pullman: Washington State University Press, 1989.

Kiang, P. N. "Bringing It All Back Home: New Views of Asian American Studies and the Community." In G. M. Nomura, R. Endo, S. H. Sumida, and R. C. Leong (eds.), *Frontiers of Asian American Studies: Writing, Research, and Commentary.* Pullman: Washington State University Press, 1989.

Kiang, P. N. "The College Experience of Southeast Asian Students." Unpublished qualifying paper, Graduate School of Education, Harvard University, 1990a.

Kiang, P. N. "A Pilot Study Examining the College Experience of Southeast Asian Refugee Students Graduating from an Urban Public University." Unpublished paper, Graduate School of Education, Harvard University, 1990b.

Kiang, P. N. "New Roots and Developing Voices: The Education of Southeast Asian Refugees at an Urban Public University." Unpublished doctoral dissertation, Graduate School of Education, Harvard University, 1991.

Lee, J. "A Study of the Needs of Asian Students: An Internship with the Asian Center." Unpublished paper, University of Massachusetts at Boston, 1987.

McClelland, K. E. "Public Platitudes and Hidden Tensions: Racial Climates at Predominantly White Liberal Arts Colleges." *Journal of Higher Education,* 1990, *61* (6), 607–642.

Morgan, J., and Mercer, J. "New Interests and Old Obstacles." *Black Issues in Higher Education,* 1990, *7* (13), 1, 12–17.

Morishita, L. M. "College Student Retention Strategies." Unpublished qualifying paper, Graduate School of Education, Harvard University, 1983.

Morse, D. "Prejudicial Studies." *Northeast—The Hartford Courant,* November 26, 1989, pp. 16–19, 24–32.

Nagasawa, R., and Espinosa, D. J. "Educational Achievement and the Adaptive Strategy of Asian American College Students: Facts, Theory, and Hypotheses." *Journal of College Student Development,* 1992, *33* (2), 137–142.

Nguyen, A. Q. "The Yale Vietnamese Community." Unpublished paper, Yale University, 1988.

Nguyen, L. H., and Halpern, J. M. (eds.). *The Far East Comes Near: Autobiographical Accounts of Southeast Asian Students in America.* Amherst: University of Massachusetts Press, 1989.

Nguyen, T. P. "Positive Self-Concept in the Vietnamese Bilingual Child." *Bilingual Journal,* Spring 1984, pp. 9–14.

Office of Policy Research and Planning. "Degrees Conferred by UMass/Boston, AY89." Boston: University of Massachusetts, 1989a.

Office of Policy Research and Planning. "Enrollment Trends at UMass/Boston, Fall 1989." Boston: University of Massachusetts, 1989b.

Office of Policy Research and Planning. "Trends in Academic Majors at UMass/Boston." Boston: University of Massachusetts, 1990.

O'Hare, W. P., and Felt, J. C. "Asian Americans: America's Fastest-Growing Minority Group." *Population Trends and Public Policy.* No. 19. Washington, D.C.: Population Reference Bureau, 1991. 221 pp. (ED 331 938)

Parmley, S. " 'The Model Minority' Myth." *Boston Globe,* August 20, 1990, pp. 1, 8–9.

Ramist, L. *College Student Attrition and Retention.* College Board Report no. 81-1. Princeton, N.J.: College Board Publications, 1981. 41 pp. (ED 200 170)

Skinner, K. A., and Hendricks, G. L. "The Shaping of Ethnic Self-Identity Among Indochinese Refugees." *Journal of Ethnic Studies,* 1979, 7 (3), 25–41.

Stage, F. K. "Research on College Students: Commonality, Difference, and Direction." *Review of Higher Education,* 1990, *13* (3), 249–258.

Suzuki, B. H. "Education and Socialization of Asian Americans: A Revisionist Analysis of the 'Model Minority' Thesis." *Amerasia Journal,* 1977, 4 (2), 23–51.

Suzuki, B. H. "Higher Education Issues in the Asian American Community." Unpublished paper, Ford Foundation, 1989.

Tinto, V. "Dropout from Higher Education: A Theoretical Synthesis of Recent Research." *Review of Educational Research,* 1975, *45* (1), 89–125.

Tinto, V. *Leaving College: Rethinking the Causes and Cures of Student Attrition.* Chicago: University of Chicago Press, 1987. 240 pp. (ED 283 416)

U.S. Commission on Civil Rights. "Recent Activities Against Citizens and Residents of Asian Descent." Washington, D.C.: U.S. Commission on Civil Rights, 1987. 99 pp. (ED 304 500)

U.S. Department of Education. "College Enrollment by Racial and Ethnic Group, Selected Years." Washington, D.C.: U.S. Department of Education, 1990.

Vang, C. "Why Are Few Hmong Women Pursuing Higher Education?" Unpublished paper, University of Colorado at Boulder, 1991.

PETER NIEN-CHU KIANG *is assistant professor in the Graduate College of Education and American Studies Program at the University of Massachusetts, Boston. He recently served as the elected East Coast representative to the national Association for Asian American Studies.*

INDEX

ABE programs, 91–92

Absenteeism, 15–18, 91

Academic achievement, 98–99; and cultural separation, 61, 62; and differences among minority students, 29–35; and low expectations for minority students, 35–36, 38–39, 40, 46, 47; and success strategies for minority students, 37–41

Administrators, 79, 92–95

Adult basic education (ABE) programs, 91–92

Adult students, 45–47; at LaGuardia Community College, 81; at Miami-Dade Community College, 71–72, 73; as new majority, 47–48; portraits of, 49–53; working with, 53–54

African American community, 15; class tensions within, 14, 17, 19–23

African American students, 36, 57, 97; and class tensions within the African American community, 14, 17, 19–23; gender tensions among, 14, 22, 23–26; at LaGuardia Community College, 81; at Miami-Dade Community College, 71; portrait of Latina of African descent, 65–69; support services for, 76–79; tensions between Caucasian students and, 14, 15–19

AIHEC. See American Indian Higher Education Consortium (AIHEC)

Alienation, 33, 60; from academic systems, 38, 56; of Asian American students, 103–104. See also Isolation

Alvarez, R., 78

American Indian Higher Education Consortium (AIHEC), 93

American Indian students, 57, 89–90; personnel commitment to, 92–95; support services for, 90–92

Anglo students. See Caucasian students

Arendt, H., 83

Aronowitz, S., 46

Asian American Resource Workshop, 102

Asian American students, 97–98; in Asian American studies courses, 104–107, 108–109; changes in gender roles for, 106–107; choices of major for, 99, 107–109; family expectations for, 101–102, 107, 109–110; identity and alienation of, 103–104; at LaGuardia Community College, 81; persistence in college by, 98–103

Assimilation, 56, 59–60

Astin, A. W., 99

Atkinson, D. R., 102–103

Attendance mode of nontraditional adults, 30, 34–35, 47–48

Attinasi, L. C., 30, 31, 99–100

Attrition, 15, 36, 99–100

Autonomy, 6

Bagasao, P., 108

Barringer, F., 97

Basic Educational Opportunity Grants (BEOG), 15–18

Belenky, M. F., 60–61, 63

Bennett, C., 36

BEOG. See Basic Educational Opportunity Grants (BEOG)

Biculturalism, 69

Black students. See African American students

Blackfeet Community College, 91, 92, 94

Bordeaux, L., 91–92

Boswell, T. D., 73

Boyer, P., 90

Brand, D., 97–98

Breaking Away (film), 13

Brophy, J. E., 36

Bryant, C., 72, 74

Butterfield, F., 97–98

Careers: relationship between education and, 30–31; and shifts in majors, 107–109

Carnegie Foundation for the Advancement of Teaching, 89, 90

Caucasian students, 68, 97; at LaGuardia Community College, 81;

ORDERING INFORMATION

NEW DIRECTIONS FOR COMMUNITY COLLEGES is a series of paperback books that provides expert assistance to help community colleges meet the challenges of their distinctive and expanding educational mission. Books in the series are published quarterly in spring, summer, fall, and winter and are available for purchase by subscription as well as by single copy.

SUBSCRIPTIONS for 1992 cost $48.00 for individuals (a savings for 20 percent over single-copy prices) and $70.00 for institutions, agencies, and libraries. Please do not send institutional checks for personal subscriptions. Standing orders are accepted.

SINGLE COPIES cost $15.95 when payment accompanies order. (California, New Jersey, New York, and Washington, D.C., residents please include appropriate sales tax.) Billed orders will be charged postage and handling.

DISCOUNTS for quantity orders are available. Please write to the address below for information.

ALL ORDERS must include either the name of an individual or an official purchase order number. Please submit your order as follows:
    Subscriptions: specify series and year subscription is to begin
    Single copies: include individual title code (such as CC1)

MAIL ALL ORDERS TO:
    Jossey-Bass Publishers
    350 Sansome Street
    San Francisco, California 94104

FOR SALES OUTSIDE OF THE UNITED STATES CONTACT:
    Maxwell Macmillan International Publishing Group
    866 Third Avenue
    New York, New York 10022

OTHER TITLES AVAILABLE IN THE
NEW DIRECTIONS FOR COMMUNITY COLLEGES SERIES
Arthur M. Cohen, Editor-in-Chief
Florence B. Brawer, Associate Editor